GIVE GOD
A
CHANCE

James
McConkey

moody press
chicago

Reprinted by permission of
Silver Publishing Society
623 Pittsburgh Life Building
Pittsburgh, Pa. 15222

Moody Press Edition, 1975

ISBN: 0-8024-2969-6

Printed in the United States of America

CONTENTS

GIVE GOD A CHANCE

Prove me now.   MALACHI 3:10

In a great city telegraph office scores of instruments were busily clicking away. Presently, in the midst of the din and clatter the door opened, and in walked a young man, a stranger. He was tall, and rather awkward, with a linen duster reaching nearly to his heels. In response to his request for employment the chief operator motioned him to a chair.

By and by another instrument began to click. The most important work of the day was at hand. The press dispatches in a distant city were ready. And by his table in that city sat one of the swiftest writers, and most skilled operators in the service, waiting to begin his rapid sending. The chief motioned to the tall young man to take his seat at the table at which the press news was to be received. He quietly did so.

The other workers lifted their heads from their instruments, to look askance at the rustic stranger as he attempted to "take" the fastest man on the line. They were watching for him to fail. But he had no notion of doing so. Answering the call, he took up his pen and began to write. And there for hour after hour he sat. Without a break, without a halt; writing a hand like a copperplate in its clearness and beauty, he tossed off sheet after sheet of copy to the waiting messenger boy, while the entire office stared in astonished admiration. When the work was finished, the position was his without any further question. To one who asked his name he replied, *Edison*. It was the beginning of his worldwide fame. All he wanted was a chance. And when he got it he did marvels.

This anecdote expresses the real thought in the verse

from Malachi cited above. "Bring ye all the tithes. . . Prove me now. . . if I will not open you the windows of heaven." What is God saying here but this? "My child, I still have windows in heaven, They are yet in service. The hinges have not grown rusty. I would rather fling them open, and pour forth, than keep them shut and hold back. I opened them for Joshua, and Jordan rolled back. I opened them for Gideon, and the hosts fled. I will open them for you, if you will only let me. On this side of the windows heaven is the same rich storehouse as of old. The fountains and streams still overflow. The treasure rooms are still bursting with gifts. The lack is not on My side. It is on yours. I am waiting. I am ready. Prove Me now. Fulfill the conditions on your part. Bring in the tithes. Give Me a chance."

Give God a chance by trusting Him.

Faith opens the soul to God. It is the channel down which God's heavenly blessings flow to us. It is the bridge which spans the chasm between heaven and earth. It is the ladder over which God's messengers of help journey to us needy earthlings. It is faith which gives God a chance to work in your life and soul. Turning away from God in unfaith is putting a plateglass between you and an electric current; it shuts off the flow of life. It is stopping your ears with cotton, so that no note of a song can float in upon your soul. It is wearing a bandage over your eyes, so that no glint of the beauty of dawn or sunset can come to your blinded vision. The life, the light, the song are there. But you shut them out. You give them no chance.

A simple illustration comes to mind here. In a human hand is an empty bottle. The bottle is under a fountain. The waters are flowing all over the bottle, but there is not a drop inside. Underneath is a legend: "Why is the bottle not filled?" The reason is simple. There is a cork in the bottle. It has no chance. Even so faith is the soul's

6

intake. Through it God's life comes in. Love is the soul's outlet. Through it God's life pours forth. To clog either is to stay the flow of life. You give God no chance. Friend, why continue to live in the shadow of death? Why has not the miracle of the new birth been wrought in your soul? Why do you, every moment, stand in jeopardy of a catastrophe which all the years of eternity can never set right? Simply because you will not fulfill God's simple conditions. You will not accept and trust Jesus Christ as the Saviour of your soul. You will not give God a chance.

Suppose the delicate mechanism of your gold watch breaks. You take it to the watchmaker and ask if he can repair it. He says he can, if you will but leave it in his hands for a few days. At once you trust him with it. For you know he can do nothing unless you give him a chance.

Or you want your portrait painted. You go to an artist friend. He tells you he will do it. But he says you must come daily to him, for so many sittings. You comply, for you know he cannot paint your portrait unless you give him a chance.

Or you go to a dock, and ask the captain of a steamship if he will land you on the other side of the ocean. He says he will, if you will buy a ticket, step aboard the boat, and trust him to carry you over. This too you do. For you know you can never cross the ocean unless you trust yourself to the ship. You must give it a chance.

How strange then, that you will not give God the same chance in eternal matters which you give to men in temporal ones! There is a breach in your soul of vastly more moment than the breakage in your watch. God will mend it if you give Him a chance. There is a picture, the image of Jesus Christ, to be painted upon your inner being, as upon every other life that would enter heaven. God will paint it if you give Him a chance.

There is a journey out into the unknown abyss of eternity, which man can only take by God's way and God's guidance. God will pilot you all the way if you give

Him a chance. Be as fair to God in matters of eternity as you are to men in the concerns of time. Fulfill His simple condition of salvation. Give yourself to Him. Trust Him, in Christ. He will surely save your soul if you only give Him a chance.

Give God a chance by praying.

There are many things too difficult for you to do. But you do not hesitate to seek someone more skillful and give him a chance to do for you. You have a precious gem to reset. You cannot do it. But you are quick to give the expert jeweler a chance to do it for you. There is a steep, dangerous mountain to climb. You do not know how to find the pathway. But you give the mountain guide a chance to lead you in it. There is a deep ford to cross. You cannot risk it. But you give the hardy ferryman the chance to pilot you across it.

It is not otherwise with you and God. There are many things you cannot do. But God says: "If ye ask I will do." There are burdens you cannot bear. Give God a chance through prayer, and He will bear them for you. There are problems too knotty for your solution. Give God a chance by prayer, and He will solve them for you. There are barriers too high for you to overleap. Ask God. They are not too high for Him. Somehow when there seems no other chance for us, prayer gives God a chance. And behold He does for us what we had forever despaired of doing ourselves.

A Christian business friend was in sore straits. A sudden demand has been made upon him for a large sum of money. Every consideration of business honor demanded its payment. Yet he was helpless to meet it. The only possible way out of the crisis seemed to be the sale of a piece of real estate. But the market was discouragingly dull. There was scarcely a buyer in it. In short, there was no human chance of selling it. So we determined to give God a chance. Spreading the whole matter before Him, we began to pray. After two weeks of earnest supplication a man came to ask our friend an offer. The latter, however, deemed it too low. So we prayed on, that God might work His perfect will in it all. At the end of six weeks of prayer the sale was made, and our friend came to us with a check for many thousands of dollars in his hand. With tears in his eyes, he said: "It seems to have come as directly from God as though He Himself had handed it to me over the counter of the bank." That was true. It was all of God. We had simply given Him a chance.

It takes God time to answer prayer.

We often fail to give God a chance in this respect. It takes time for God to paint a rose. It takes time for God to grow an oak. It takes time for God to make bread from a wheat field. He takes the earth. He pulverizes. He softens. He enriches. He wets with showers and dews. He warms with life. He gives the blade, the stock, the amber grain, and then at last the bread for the hungry. All this takes time. Therefore we sow, and till, and wait, and trust, until all God's purpose has been wrought out. We give God a chance in this matter of time. We need to learn this same lesson in our prayer life. It takes God time to answer prayer.

A Christian worker had reached the end of the week, well wearied with service. The sunshine and rippling river were luring him to an hour's rowing. Boarding a passing car he was soon on his way to the river bank. As he neared it he remembered that it was late in the season, and there was a likelihood of the boathouse being closed. But the outing for tired nerves and weary body seemed a clear need. So he lifted his heart quietly in prayer that if it were the Lord's will He might send along the caretaker of the boathouse to furnish the boat. Reaching the spot he found to his disappointment that the house was closed.

Turning to leave under the impulse of the moment, the thought flashed in, "It has only been a moment or two since you prayed the Lord to send along the boatman, and now you are going away without even waiting long enough for him to get here. Why don't you give God a chance?" So he sat down by the river bank to wait. In ten minutes the boatkeeper came strolling along. The house was opened, the boat secured, and the refreshing of an hour's outing enjoyed to the full. With it came another simple lesson in the prayer life, that it takes God time to answer prayer, and that we therefore need to give God a chance.

Take this matter of conversion. You have an unsaved loved one. You have prayed for him for months, for years. He is still outside the kingdom. God has not answered your prayer, you say. But perhaps you are at sea in your view of conversion. Does God bring a soul into His kingdom as you might lift a child over a hedge, or hurl a stone across a stream? Does man's choice have no place in this? It surely does. It matters not by what theological sidepath you approach this matter of conversion. One thing is certain, however. God may *move* upon man's will, but He does not *supplant* that will. Whatever may be the mystery of God's choice, no soul ever comes into the kingdom without his own choice.

Hence concerning the conversion of a resisting soul remember this: God is striving with a human will. But do you know what it is to move upon a human will? This very loved one you have warned. With him you have pleaded. With him you have reasoned. Yet all these years that strong will has resisted you. Now, at the last, you have given up in sheer despair the attempt to move upon a human will. Do you not realize then what it means for God to do it? God may have heart-idols to overthrow. God may have to foil chosen plans. God may allow afflictions to come. God must press in upon the man engrossed in the temporal, a growing vision of the eternal. God must needs cherish, woo, disappoint, uplift, bereave, en-

10

rich, impoverish, yea, bring to bear a multitude of influences upon a resisting will, ere it yields to Him. But to unstop ears deaf to the voice of God, to open eyes blind to the vision of God, to turn aside wandering feet into the path of God, all this takes time. Therefore, give God a chance.

Give God a chance by yielding.

God can do nothing with us if we do not yield. He has no chance.

We recall a day of sight-seeing in the palaces of Genoa. From room to room we had followed the caretaker in his tour. Paintings, sculpture, curios of all sorts had followed each other in rapid train. Finally we entered a room seemingly empty. Bare walls, floors, and tables greeted us. Presently the guide led us across the room to the wall at the farther side. There we espied a niche in the wall. It was covered with a glass case. Behind the case was a magnificent violin, in perfect preservation. This, said the guide, was Paganini's favorite violin; the rich old Cremona upon which he loved most of all to display his marvelous skill.

We gazed intently upon the superb instrument, with its warm, rich tints, sinuous curves, and perfect model, listening meanwhile to the estimate of its almost priceless value. And then we tried to imagine the wondrous strains the touch of the great master would bring forth if he were there in that quiet palace chamber. Then came the thought: Nay, but this could not be. For it would not matter what rich melodies were in the inner soul of the master. It would not avail how eager he might be to pour them forth in sweetest, tenderest strain through that magnificent instrument. He could not possibly do so. For it was locked up against him. It was an unyielded instrument. It was like thousands of lives which are padlocked against God, not back of a fragile, easily shattered glass case, but behind the impenetrable armor of an unyielded human will. *It gave the master no chance.*

Friend, is this why your life seems barren and fruitless? Is this why God does not seem to be using that life? Is it that, however willing, He cannot use it because it is unyielded to Him? For this picture of an instrument is no fancy, but the very one God employs in His Word. "Present your members as instruments to God," He says. But how can He use an unpresented instrument? The very word "present" pictures the secret of your trouble. It means "to place near the hand" of one; to set at the hand of another as one might set a tool or instrument. To be a surrendered man, a yielded man, is simply to be God's *handyman*. The carpenter is at work. Some of his tools are hanging on the wall of his workshop. Some are right at hand on his workbench. When he wants one quickly and urgently which will he use? The one he can reach quickest, the one "set at his hand." This is precisely where God wants your life. Not hanging on the wall of selfishness, but yielded, reachable, usable. This is what gives God a chance.

Moses, with his hesitation and stammering tongue, seemed to be a weak instrument. But he gave God a chance. And God made him the lawgiver and leader of His people. Gideon looked with fear and trembling upon the great work before him. Yet he gave God a chance. And God routed a great and mighty host with his puny lamps and pitchers. David was but a stripling shepherd, shut up in obscurity. But he gave God a chance. And God brought him to a throne. The little lad with the loaves and fishes had but a mite. But he gave God a chance. And the Master broke and broke the morsels until a famishing multitude was fed before the wondering eyes of the grateful boy. The man on the Damascus road gave God a chance on that fateful day. And God shook the world with him. Seven weary fishermen peered through the morning gloaming upon the form of one standing upon the shore. The night was far spent. The day was at hand. The hour for successful fishing was past. But when the voice rang out over the waters, "Cast the net on the right side of the ship," they yielded to the Master. And He gave them such a catch as they had never known in all their fisher days when they gave Him the chance.

It is not how much do you have, but how much of yours does God have? It is not a question of bemoaning what you have not, but of yielding what you have. One talent yielded is worth more than ten simply possessed. Is your handful of grain in the hands of the sower? That bit yielded is worth more than a bin hoarded. The nugget of gold, which has been minted and coined, and is purchasing hourly blessing as it passes from hand to hand, is worth all the undug tons of treasure which the earth conceals.

Reader, you have given pleasure a chance. Has it paid? You are giving ambition a chance. Does it satisfy? You are giving money-getting a chance. Is it for self or God? Have a care. When life comes to an end is it going to be ashes—emptiness—fruitlessness? What a pity! Try God. Give Him a chance. What is your life, anyhow? Where is it centered? Only for time? Sit down and think, not only about your soul but your life. Ask yourself not necessarily what God's judgment will be, but what your own honest verdict upon your life will be if it goes on to the finish exactly as it is now. Any Christian man who will do that honestly, will begin to live for God. He will see that an immortal life which does not take into account God's eternal plan for it must be a failure.

Friend, when you come to the end where the world will have shriveled to its true littleness, and eternity looms up to its real bigness; when the things which are seen are really found to be temporal and the things which are unseen, eternal; when you are on the brink of stepping over into the glory where God is all and in all; then you will be glad, oh, so glad, that today, when you finished this message, you laid it down and decided that as for you and your life, from this time forth you would *give God a chance.*

FAITH

For ye are all the children of God by faith in Christ Jesus.　　　GALATIANS 3:26

The Word of God does not much concern itself with definitions of faith. But it is often illustrating and picturing faith. And none of its pictures is simpler or more beautifully clear than that one in Hebrews 12:2.

Faith is "looking unto Jesus," not simply looking at Jesus.

There is a so-called faith which looks *at* Jesus, instead of looking *unto* Him. And there are many people who are thus simply looking at Him. They believe in Jesus as a historical personage. They admit the surpassing beauty of His life. They say no man can match His incomparable teachings. They say, "I believe in Jesus Christ as surely as you do." But they believe in Him with the head, not with the heart. They hold Him up and scrutinize His beauty as one might gaze through a microscope upon some lovely specimen of nature's handiwork. They see the picture which the Word of God has drawn of His only begotten Son and they are driven to confess, as they gaze, that the world has never looked upon such a matchless character, before or since. But they never go any farther. They utterly fail to realize how far this sort of faith falls short of the faith which is needed to save a soul from eternal death. They are merely looking at Jesus as they look at any other individual who has loomed up on the horizon of the past. But that is not enough. You may believe in Jesus with that sort of faith and never be saved. You may

14

confess with that sort of confession yet be forever shut out of the kingdom of Heaven. You may look at Jesus here, never see His face in the glory hereafter. The devils themselves believe with that sort of faith. Yet it is not a belief which saves but a belief which trembles. You must go farther than this to find the faith which saves, for

Faith, the faith which saves, is looking unto Jesus.

There is a vast difference here. And wherein does it lie? Exactly what is it to look *unto* Jesus, with the faith that saves the soul? Let us illustrate. You owe a thousand dollars. You give your creditor a note for it. That note is endorsed by a rich friend. Suppose it to be in the days when imprisonment for debt is in force. By and by you become bankrupt. Not one dollar do you have to meet your obligation. As the day approaches upon which your note falls due your creditor begins to harass you. He exacts every dollar. He threatens you with imprisonment if you fail to pay. Straightway your heart is filled with anxious care. You cannot possibly pay the debt. As the hour draws near your distress of soul grows almost unbearable as you think of the suffering of your loved ones whom you have unwittingly involved in your fate. But now you remember that you have a kind friend as endorser on your note. You go to him in your crisis. At once he says, "My friend, do not worry one moment longer. I am your endorser on this note. I have ample assets to meet it. Just look to me to pay it."

At once your whole attitude changes. You leave off worrying. Peace fills your heart. Another man has taken the whole burden. And thus it is lifted entirely from you. You have ceased to try. You simply trust. That is, you are looking to another, and to him alone to pay your debt. Hold before your mind this thought of a man looking to his endorser to pay his note. Hold it there not for one moment but for several. Hold it until you have a sharp, clear picture of what your attitude of mind would be if

15

you were thus depending upon a friend to pay your note. Do you grasp it clearly? Can you think it through? Can you put yourself exactly in that place? Have you held it there now until there is no blur nor fog to the mental picture of just how you would look to an endorser to pay your note? Well, that is *faith*.

Faith is depending.

Surely. That is exactly what looking to another means. That is precisely what the maker of the note does toward his endorser. It is relying upon another. It is counting upon him. It is throwing your weight upon him and his word. It is depending upon him to do the very thing he has promised. You wish to send your little child down a street in the city. A friend offers to take her in charge. You give her into his keeping, saying, "I look to you to take care of my child." You simply mean that you depend upon him to do it. You break a limb by accident. Your friend the surgeon comes to set it. You say, "Doctor, I look to you to set that limb aright." You are about to take a journey. You take your seat in the train. You say to the conductor, "Friend, I look to you to bring me to my destination." In all these cases where you are looking to others you mean that you are depending upon them. You are counting upon them to do the thing in question, and are making no effort whatever to do it yourself. This is exactly what looking to Jesus for salvation is. He is a specialist in saving men. That is His business and His alone. "He shall save His people from their sins." Therefore you are to look to Him, count upon Him, depend upon Him to save your soul just as simply, helplessly, and absolutely as you, a bankrupt debtor, would depend upon your rich endorser to pay your note. And when a man passes from this looking at Jesus as a historical personage, to this dependent looking to Jesus to save his soul, he passes from the faith of the devils who believe and tremble, to the faith of God's sons who believe and are saved.

Faith is looking away from everything else unto Jesus.

This word "looking unto" has a meaning which is not expressed in our own version of the Bible. It means not only looking unto but looking away. *"Off*-looking *unto* Jesus," is the rendering in Luther's translation. The man who is looking unto one thing or person must look away from everything else. When you trust another to guide you on a dark night you look away from your own knowledge of the way unto his. When you put yourself under the instruction of a great teacher you look away from your own ignorance unto his wisdom. When in weakness you lean upon the strong arm of a friend you look *away* from your own helplessness unto his strength. So when you look to Jesus for salvation you must look to Him alone. You look away from your own merits, away from your own efforts and strugglings, away from your own self-righteousness—unto Jesus. Especially is it true that

Faith is looking away from your own works unto Jesus.

It is Jesus who saves. And faith is looking unto Him for salvation. Therefore we need to steadily look away from our own works—unto Jesus. Nothing in the Word of God is clearer than this. "We reckon therefore that a man is justified by faith, apart from the works of the law." (Ro 3:28, RV). "But to him that worketh not, but believeth on him that justifieth the ungodly, his faith is reckoned for righteousness" (Ro 4:5). "Blessing upon the man, unto whom God reckoneth righteousness apart from works" (Ro 4:6, RV).

And why does God lay such stress upon our looking away from works unto Jesus in order to be saved? Simply because the state of the lost soul is such that good works utterly fall short of meeting that soul's supreme need. For consider a moment these two great facts concerning the unsaved soul.

17

The unsaved man has a sin-stained past.

The unsaved man is condemned to death.

How wholly insufficient are good works to meet this dual need of the soul. Will a good deed wash away guilt? Can acts of charity cleanse the blood-stained past? Can works of mercy purge a conscience crimsoned with sin? Can anything a man may do or be atone for sin? Nay, "without shedding of blood there is no remission" (Heb 9:22). Jesus is our only sin bearer. Jesus alone is the purger of the soul from guilt. We must look away from works unto Him alone. And so too of the sentence of death upon every lost soul because of sin. "The soul that sinneth, it shall die" (Eze 18:4,20). Can any good deed lift a soul out from under the awful shadow of its sentence of death? Though we give our bodies to be burned, will that do it? Though we bestow all our goods to feed the poor, will that do it? Will a genial disposition, or a kind heart, or a loving ministry to the suffering and needy, will these do it? Nay. A lofty purpose, a moral life, a kind heart, can never lift that condemnation from the guilty soul. But Jesus can lift it. For He Himself has suffered the death sentence. He has suffered it in our place. And he who believeth in the Lord Jesus Christ "shall not come into condemnation; but is passed from death unto life" (Jn 5:24). Again

Faith is looking away from your own faith unto Jesus.

Some people try to have faith in their own faith, instead of faith in Jesus Christ. They keep looking for a subjective condition. They ought to be looking to an objective Christ. True faith pays no attention whatever to itself. It centers all its gaze upon Christ. For faith is not our savior. Faith is simply an attitude of the soul through which Jesus saves. When Satan cannot beguile us in any other way he gets us to scrutinizing our faith, instead of looking unto Christ. That man has the strongest heart who is the least conscious of its existence. And that faith is the strongest which pays no attention to itself. You may weaken the heart by centering your anxious attention upon it. So nothing will quicker weaken faith than the constant endeavor to discover it. It is like the child's digging up of the seed to see if it is growing. It is a curiosity which brings disaster to the seed. It is not a man's faith, but his faith in Christ which saves him. To be looking unto Christ is faith. To be looking unto anything else, even unto faith, is a trouble to the soul.

And is not this the deep and real significance of our Lord's comparison of faith with the mustard seed? When He tells us of the power that will come to us if we have faith as a grain of mustard seed, what does He mean? Surely not that we are to have only a little faith. For He always rebukes "little faith." But rather He is saying this: "Hold or regard your faith as you regard, and look upon the grain of mustard seed." And how is that? Why does Christ choose so trifling a symbol of faith as the mustard seed? Because He is contrasting faith and God. The emphasis of His teaching here is not on the "have faith," but on "have faith *in God*." He is turning our eyes toward faith. He is turning our faith toward God. And so nothing but the tiniest and most insignificant of seeds could symbolize the utter littleness, yea nothingness of faith, as compared with the omnipotent God who works through our faith. But how else is faith like the mustard seed? Plainly in this. That each, however insignificant in itself, is the channel of life through which flows the life of God. The wonder of faith, and the wonder of the mustard seed is the same. It is that though nothing in themselves God can, and does, work through them.

Therefore do not worry about your faith. Do not always be scanning it. Look away from it altogether—unto Jesus. For faith alone is naught. It is only faith *in Jesus* that counts. Take care that you are depending upon Jesus to save. And faith will take care of itself.

19

Faith is not clinging, it is letting go.

Somewhere we have read a story like this. A traveler upon a lonely road was set upon by bandits who robbed him of his all. They then led him into the depths of the forest. There, in the darkness, they tied a rope to the limb of a great tree, and bade him catch hold of the end of it. Swinging him out into the blackness of surrounding space, they told him he was hanging over the brink of a giddy precipice. The moment he let go he would be dashed to pieces on the rocks below. And then they left him. His soul was filled with horror at the awful doom impending. He clutched despairingly the end of the swaying rope. But each dreadful moment only made his fate more sure. His strength steadily failed. At last he could hold on no longer. The end had come. His clenched fingers relaxed their convulsive grip. He fell—*six inches,* to the solid earth at his feet! It was only a ruse of the robbers to gain time in escaping. And when he let go it was not to death, but to the safety which had been waiting him through all his time of terror.

Friend, clutching will not save you. It is only Satan's trick to keep you from being saved. And all the while is your heart not full of fear? *Let go!* That is God's plan to save you. "And will I not fall to death?" you say. Nay. Underneath is—*Jesus!* He is the Rock of your salvation. And when in sheer helplessness you let go, and fall upon Him; fear goes, and death goes, and safety comes forever. For He, not your clinging, "He shall save His people from their sins" (Mt 1:21).

Faith is not trying; it is ceasing.

A drowning man was struggling in the water. On the shore stood his wife in an agony of fright and grief. By her side stood an onlooker, seemingly indifferent to the man's fate. Again and again did the suffering woman appeal to him to save her husband. But he made no move. By and by the desperate struggles of the man be-

20

gan to abate. He was losing strength. Presently he arose to the surface, weak and helpless. At once the onlooker leaped into the stream and brought the man in safety to the shore. "Why did you not save my husband sooner?" cried the now grateful woman. "Madam, I could not save your husband so long as he struggled. He would have dragged us both to certain death. But when he grew weak, and ceased to struggle, then it was easy to save him."

To struggle to save ourselves is simply to hinder Christ from saving us. To come to the place of faith we must pass from the place of effort to the place of accepted helplessness. Our very efforts to save ourselves turn us aside from that attitude of helpless dependence upon Christ which is the one attitude we need to take in order that He may save us. It is only when we cease from our own works and depend thus helplessly upon Him that we realize how perfectly able He is to save without any aid from us.

Faith is not doing; it is resting.

When work is ended then comes rest. So is it with the work of redemption. Jesus has finished that work. He has borne our sins. He has died in our place. Therefore on Calvary He cried out, "It is finished." And it is ours now to rest, for the work is done. "Rest in the Lord" is the word for us. But what does a man do when he rests? He does not do anything. He quits doing. He throws his weary body on a chair, a couch, a bed, and lets that hold him. He ceases all trying to hold himself. And so what do you do when you rest in Christ for salvation? You do not do anything. You throw yourself, your weight, on Christ and let Him do. You simply—rest. For while you are trying you are not resting. And when you begin to rest, you cease trying. Wherefore "we which have believed do enter into rest" (Heb 4:3). And the man who believes in Christ does indeed rest in Him for the salvation of his soul.

21

Faith is not feeling; it is taking God's Word.

In a gospel meeting a penitent woman was seeking salvation. The evangelist quoted to her anxious soul those precious words of Isaiah 53:6: "The Lord hath laid on Him (Christ) the iniquity of us all." He showed her that though she was a sinner and had gone astray like a lost sheep, yet God's word clearly stated that all her sins had been laid upon Jesus Christ. "The Lord" had done this apart from any feeling or emotion of hers. All she need do was to take God's word and depend upon Christ for this remission of sin. She seemingly did so, and went home rejoicing. The next morning she came downstairs with tears in her eyes. The old burden of anxiety for sins had come back. Her little boy, who had been with her in the meeting the night before, noticed her grief. "Mamma, what is troubling you?" "Oh, last night I *felt* I was saved. But this morning it all seems like a dream. I fear I am deceived." "Mamma," said the little lad, "get your Bible and turn to Isaiah 53:6." And she did so, and read, "The Lord hath laid on him the iniquity of us all." "Mamma, is the verse still there?" "Yes, my son." "Then your sins were laid on Jesus," said the wise lad. The mother saw the truth. She took God's word, without regard to her feelings. And then God's peace came to stay.

Friend, your salvation rests not upon your changeable feelings, but upon God's unchangeable fact. That fact of God is that Christ has borne your sins, and has died in your place. No feeling of yours, whether of joy or grief, exultation or despondency, peace or distress, can possibly affect that great fact. Therefore let not one fragment of your faith hinge upon your own moods or emotions. But let it rest implicitly in God's word. For in that and that alone will it find perfect peace.

The day you turn your face from sin to God; the day you look away from your own works, your own feelings, even your own faith—unto Jesus; the day you cease *clinging, struggling, and trying; the day you see that faith is simply depending upon Jesus as a bankrupt debtor depends upon his endorser; the day you begin to so depend upon and confess Christ as your Saviour; that day God will save your soul, and through that selfsame simple faith will make you—*A SON OF GOD.

THE NEW COMMANDMENT

A new commandment I give unto you that ye love one another. JOHN 13:34

There is a beautiful tradition of the last days of the apostle John. He had gathered together his disciples for a parting message. As he looked into their faces with all the tenderness of the parting moment, he said to them, "Little children, love one another." But they said, "John, we have heard that message before. You have been telling us that *from the beginning*. Give us some other word." And looking down upon them, he said, with increased tenderness, "Little children, that which ye have heard *from the beginning* that speak I unto you, that ye love one another." "Ah!" they replied, "but you have been giving us that message ever since we have known you. Now that you are going away we want some parting word by which to remember you. Give us some *new* commandment tonight, dear John." And then for the last time he said, "Little children, dear little children, *a new commandment* I give unto you, that ye love one another." He had no other commandment. All of the commandments were bound up in that one great bundle of love and obedience, that we love not ourselves, but love others, as Jesus our Lord has loved us.

Let us plunge then into the heart of our subject of the love life.

The Kindness of Love

"Love suffereth long and is kind." And what is this kindness of love? It is this: That no matter how much love is ill-treated or scorned; how much it is ignored or neglected; how little return or requital is made to it, yet it suffers all these things and stays kind. It is the fixedness of love amid all sorts of slights and lack of appreciation. It is the ceaseless lovingness of love regardless of how people mistreat it.

I was sitting one day in the home of a Christian woman. Suddenly there came a knock at the door. She opened it, and there stood a tramp asking for food. As it happened she had nothing but bread and butter in the house, which she promptly gave him. He passed through the gate, walked to the edge of the sidewalk, and threw the bread into the gutter. She saw the act from the window, and turning to me said, "There, that is the last tramp I will ever feed." She had love enough to give to one who seemed to be in need. But when that love was flouted, when it was mistreated, it could not stay kind, it could not abide. What then does God mean here by the love that suffereth long and stays kind? It is like this:

One morning away down in sunny Italy, I awoke conscious that my bedroom was heavy with the fragrance of heliotrope. I arose and searched my room. I could not see a spray nor a blossom anywhere. I walked to the casement and opened the shutter and the mystery was revealed. There, growing like a climber, was a magnificent bush of heliotrope laden with a mass of beautiful blooms. All night long its locks had been wet with the dews of the night, but still it poured forth its fragrance. All night long its tendrils had been chilled with the cold mountain airs, but still it poured forth its life. All night its beauty had been hidden in the enshrouding darkness, but it withheld not one atom of its fragrance. No eye beheld its beauty; no soul was ravished by its exquisite perfume. What a neglect! How shameful such treatment seemed to be! But what of that! Was it not a heliotrope? Had not God made it to send forth fragrance? And why should it not continue to pour it forth whether man slept or waked? And so all unseen, unsensed, unappreciated, it kept pouring out its wealth of fragrance, filling every nook and corner of the sleeper's room with the ceaseless outpouring of its own life of sweet-scentedness.

Behold the love of God! Behold the kind of love God Himself would live through us! A love which keeps on loving despite all neglect. Yet, here is the difference between the fine gold of God's love, and the common clay of our human love. We *have* love, but it flees away when ill-treated or neglected. God *is* love. And, like the heliotrope with its wealth of fragrance, God pours out the riches of His love unceasingly upon all, in divine regardlessness of their neglect of Him. We love men so long as they make some return of that love. But God loves men because they *need* love. We are kind to those who show some gratitude and appreciation. But "He is kind to the unthankful and the evil."

"Love suffereth long and is kind." Mark that fine phrase *is kind*. The beaten gold of a precious truth lies hidden in those two words. You know those test days which come into our lives. Everything seems awry and atwist; everything going wrong. We go about the house with clenched teeth, set lips, and knit brows bearing our trials. We "suffer long." But we are anything but kind within. And yet just here lies the victory. For victory is not simply in our long suffering of burdens and trials, but the inner spirit of kindness which we persist in cherishing toward those who are causing us to suffer.

The Coveringness of Love

Love "beareth all things." (1 Co 13:7). But the word literally is "*covereth* all things." What does that mean? Away down in the depths of the natural human heart is a tendency to uncover the frailties and foibles of our fellow man; to hold them up to the light of day, "to the scorn and criticism of those who gaze in idle curiosity upon them." But *that* is not love. It is this deceitful heart of

26

ours. What on the other hand does love do? Do you remember that story of the friends who brought the paralytic to Jesus? When they could not get near Him because of the press, they took off the roof and let him down into the Lord's presence. This word "beareth" in verse 7 is the same Greek root as the word, "to take the roof off," only this word means, "to put a roof over." And that is what love does. It puts a roof over, instead of taking the roof off, the frailties and weaknesses of our fellowmen. *The greatest incentive to practice a Christ-like grace toward others is to remember how God has poured forth that same grace upon us.* That is a splendid rule here. Are you tempted to uncover the shortcomings of your fellows? Is censoriousness a besetting sin with you? And would you learn the secret of victory over it? It lies here. The instant you are tempted to uncover another's life remember how God in His grace has covered yours with the blood of Jesus Christ. Think of the years of sin and rebellion; think of the wasted time and strength; think of the coldness and lovelessness when the heart should have been warm with love; think of the sins of omission and commission; think of all your unfaithfulness, waywardness, and selfishness. And then consider how quickly God has covered all these sins! How quickly the crimson flood swept over them! How completely they are buried in the oblivion of the past! How quickly they were sunk in the sea! As you remember how God has done all this for your weak and guilty past you will be ashamed of the unChrist-like spirit which uncovers instead of covers. Your heart will come to cherish that tender word of the great apostle, "And be ye kind to one another, tenderhearted, forgiving one another, even as God for Christ's sake hath forgiven you" (Eph 4:32). God is asking you to have not the malice which uncovers, but the love which covers the frailties of others. Do not be one of those who take the roof off, but one of those who put the roof over the weaknesses of your fellows.

The Practicalness of Love

"Little children, let us love in *deed* and in *truth*" (1 Jn 3:18). What does John mean? If you and I were drawing the picture of love the first and natural thought with us would be the emotion of love, the tender sentiment of love in the heart, the feeling of love that is there. Now, not for one moment would I disparage the conscious glow and zeal, the ardor of love in the heart. But I am glad that when God comes to give us a test of love it is something so practical and so simple. For God does not anywhere in this wonderful chapter make emotional consciousness the test of love, but definitely says that we are to love in *deed*. What does He mean? This: Love is doing; it is serving; it is helping; it is ministering. The test of love is not the glow of love in our hearts, but the deeds of love in our lives. "He that keepeth my commandment, *he* it is that loveth me." "Simon, son of Jonas, lovest thou me? Yea, Lord, thou knowest that I love thee." "Well, Peter, love consists not in your ardent protestations; not in your transient feelings. There is something else, Peter, do you love me? Do something. Feed My sheep. Prove it in your life, in your acts."

Now, that is a precious thought and for this reason. We are not all high-keyed along emotional lines. We do not all have the intense, inner consciousness of love that a man like the apostle Paul had. Some of us are work-a-day, practical men and women, who live our daily life in the will of God and in daily faithfulness, not always with special experience of the inner passion of love. How comforting to know that if our daily life is unselfish and helpful, and we are living it for God and others as best we know, then we are living this blessed love-life as surely as the man who is more constantly sensible of the inner burnings of love in his soul. Wherefore if when we sing "More love to Thee, O Christ," we grow discouraged at the seeming lack of it, let us remember that the final test of love is not how we feel, but how we live. And that explains the teaching of love for our enemies. One says, "How can I do that? I do not feel that love toward them which I have toward my dear ones." The Lord does not expect it. The test here is the same test of deeds. If he were hungry would you feed him? If he were thirsty would you give him drink? If he were drowning would you throw him a line? Certainly you would. You love Jesus Christ too much for anything else. Well, that is the test of love to enemies. Jesus Himself says so, and we can live that love-life toward any man even though he be one who declares himself our foe.

The Suffering of Love

As said before, if you and I were drawing this picture we would think about the ardor, the glow, the sentiment of love in the heart. But the very climax of love is what it will *suffer*. When you think of the love of the Lord Jesus Christ, what do you think most perfectly voices it? Is it His words as a teacher, wonderful as they are? Is it His deeds of love and mercy, gracious as they were? Is it His tender compassion in that wonderful scene of weeping over Jerusalem, wondrous as the emotion of it was? Nay, it is not in these. When you want to see the highest love of Jesus Christ you picture Gethsemane, the hall of scourging, or the dark hill where he hung between a compassionate heaven and an uncompassionate earth. The picture of Jesus Christ, which melts our hearts in love, is the picture of what He suffered for us. The highest proof of love is suffering. Therefore a man or woman may live on the loftiest plane of the love-life, and yet not always have the conscious *feeling* of love accompanying it. May I prove it? There never was a time in the life of our Lord when He had less of the *feeling* of love than when He hung on the cross. Why? Because that was a time when hanging there as a substitute for you and me, as a sin offering, God Himself must needs turn away His face and the overmastering emotion of Christ's heart was expressed in that cry: "My God! My God! Why hast thou

29

forsaken Me?" Despair and agony were the emotions that occupied and overmastered the heart of Jesus Christ at that moment. There was never a time when He had less of the emotion of love. Yet there never was a time when He loved us more. Even so some of you are bearing, for the Master's sake, burdens of weary toil, sorrows and sins of others, censure and misrepresentation, bitter estrangements, cherished hopes deferred for weary years, patient faith which has not yet issued into sight. You, I say, who are bearing these without any special inner consciousness or feeling of love, are yet living the highest form of love a man or woman can live for Jesus Christ. For the highest expression of love is suffering. And he who brings to his Master the scars of his suffering for His name and His kingdom lays at His feet the loftiest tribute, even as it is the costliest sacrifice, which love can bring to the master of his heart. "Greater love hath no man than this, that a man lay down his life" (Jn 15:13), that a man suffer, for this Friend.

The All-Sufficiency of Love

"Love is the fulfilling of the law" (Ro 13:10). They say there are thirty thousand promises in the Book. I suppose there are nearly as many commands and precepts. Perhaps you are tempted to say, "Then I can never keep God's law and live in His will. If God would only have some simple rule of the Christian life that would fulfill everything!" Well, God has. "Love is the fulfilling of the law." If you love a man you will not steal from him; you will not murder him; you will not covet his goods; you will not bear false witness against him; if you love a man you are fulfilling—you are *filling full* the law. Some of you are husbands and fathers. If the legislature should pass a hundred statutes concerning the care of your wives and children, you men would not only do all the legislators enact, but you would do a thousand things they never would think of putting on the statute books.

Why? Because you *love* your wife and children. You would not only keep the law, but you would *fill full* the law to overflowing. Now, that is God's simple rule of life for you and me. As we come to the twilight of this day, as we sit down in the evening hour to meditate over it, we do not have to think of all the commandments that are in the Book. We simply say to ourselves, "The words that I spoke this day, were they in love? The deeds that I did, were they in love? That letter I wrote, was it in love? All I have done this day, can I lay God's straight edge of love along side of it?" How simple that makes the Christian life! For the man or woman who lives that simple law of love is fulfilling God's great purpose in this life.

But someone asks, "Can we ever have such love; is it possible to gain such love?" Let us note, in answer, three thoughts about the *obtainment* of love.

The Desirableness of Love

"Follow after love" (1 Co 14:1), says the great apostle. Make it your goal. Make it the pursuit and passion of your life. Mark its dizzy height—"the greatest of all." It is the pinnacle of all Christian grace. It is the charm, the crown of all Christian character. It is the very nature, the very life of God Himself within you. For "He that loveth not knoweth not God; for God is love" (1 Jn 4:8). Set it ever before you as your goal. Think much upon it. Pray for it. Be jealous of all that dims or hinders it. Bridle the haste of your tongue. Banish the unkindness from your voice. Curb the injustice of your judgments. Frown upon criticism of others. Flee harshness and unlovingness as you would heinous sins of the flesh. Be not disheartened in your seeking. That which is the golden crown and jewel of all character is worth the patient, continuous seeing which these words "follow after" hint at.

The Source of Love

"The fruit of the Spirit is love," (Gal 5:22). There hangs a peach. Note its gorgeous coloring. Mark it ripened lusciousness. But have you thought how long it took God to ripen that peach? There was the planted seed. It burst, and from it came the seedling tree. It grew apace until in time came the first blossom, and then the tiny fruit, and then the wind, the sunshine, the showers, and the ripening, until there hangs the luscious peach. It took God a long while to make that fruit. Even so love is *the fruit* of the spirit. Be patient with yourself as to this matchless fruitage of the Spirit. It takes time for God to make us bear a ripened fruit in our hearts and lives; and love is such a fruit.

"The fruit of the Spirit is love." My natural heart does not love. That is, it does not love God. It does not love lost men. It does not love the world that lies in darkness. It loves the baubles, the prizes, and the pleasures of this world. Nor does it matter how hard I try to love God and the things of God. I cannot make my natural heart do it. Can you? Have you and I not failed, oh, so often here? But now if God could only take the spirit of a lover, and put it into your heart, and mine, we would love. Because a lover loves without trying. He loves instinctively, spontaneously, out-flowingly. And this is just what God did when He begot us in Christ Jesus. "Because ye are sons, God hath sent forth the Spirit of His Son into your hearts" (Gal 4:6). He put into our hearts the spirit of the greatest Lover in the universe—the spirit of Jesus Christ Himself. And would you know then the secret of fulness of love? It is simply the secret of the Spirit. Believe in the Spirit's indwelling; yield to the Spirit; pray in the Spirit; walk in the Spirit; serve in the Spirit—yea, learn to live in the Spirit. For all you do to foster and cherish His life within you will bring you richness and fulness of the blessed love life. And all that chills and grieves Him in your daily life will surely dim and quench the love within which is the fruit He is seeking day by day to ripen and develop in your innermost soul.

The Eternalness of Love

Faith shall pass away because it shall at last climax in sight. Hope shall cease. For what a man seeth doth he yet hope for? Knowledge itself—or rather the gift—"shall vanish away." "For now we see through a glass, darkly" (1 Co 13:12). We are like men looking at the sun through a bit of smoked glass. When, face to face, we behold the splendor of the Sun of Righteousness we will throw away the clouded glass. Yea, and our knowledge without love "profiteth nothing." For the humblest washwoman who lives the love life for God will find up there a priceless and imperishable inheritance, while the most learned sage though he has a wealth of knowledge, yet knows not love, will find himself stripped of his assets, a bankrupt in the court of God. So then all these gifts will pass away. But there is one treasure every fragment of which laid up here reaches over into, and abides through the endless ages of eternity. And that is love.

You may sit all alone in the great Dresden gallery, in an isolated room dedicated wholly to one great painting, the Sistine Madonna. You may gaze for hours upon its wondrous picture of tender, majestic motherhood. Yet when Raphael's masterpiece has faded into oblivion the cup of cold water you yesterday gave in the love of your Lord will live forever. You may stand in a single famous chamber in the Vatican gallery where there are four of the world's greatest masterpieces of sculpture. Men call it the most priceless center of art in the world. Yet when Laocoon, with all its writhing agony, and the Apollo Belvidere, the most faultless carving of the human form in existence, have crumbled into dust, and even the names of their creators have been forgotten, then that humble deed of love you did today, unseen by any eye save that of God, shall abide forever. Yea, when all the waves of human fame, human applause and human flattery have died away upon the sands of time, the tiny wave of love you started in some kind word, some loving ministry, will be rolling and breaking upon the shores of eternity. Every song that floats from your lips in the spirit of love; every word of comfort to the sorrowing; every loving warning and admonition to the wayward; every prayer that goes up out of the love of your heart for a friend in need; every word of cheer and solace to the despondent one; every bit of suffering from criticism and misrepresentation borne in the spirit of love; every mite of silver and gold given for the love of the Master and His suffering ones—every such deed of love, however insignificant it may seem to you, will meet you at the throne of reward, and go with you in your shining train of influence and love all through the countless millenniums of eternity. And does there come a time when your voice of love is silent, your hand of love motionless, your human heart of love no longer throbs, and men say, "He is dead?" Then shall come a voice from heaven saying, "Blessed are the dead which die in the Lord. . . their works do follow them" (Rev 14:13). Would you build not for time but for a deathless eternity? Then build in love, upon the foundation of Christ Jesus. For so doing you built not that "wood, hay, and stubble," which consume away in the searching fires of God's great test day, but that "gold, silver, and precious stones," which shall only shine forth in greater preciousness and splendor in that same day of revelation of all things.

PRAYER

If ye ask ... I will do.   JOHN 14:14

It is a wonderful promise.

Many and precious are the promises which God gives to His praying children. He tells us that as we pray and receive our joy shall be full, (Jn 16:24); that if we bring all things to Him in prayer His own unspeakable peace shall possess and keep our hearts in Christ Jesus, (Phil 4:7); that of all who ask from Him not one shall be turned away; that to any who knock at His door it shall without fail be opened, (Mt 7:7-8). Familiar enough and gracious too is His truth that as we ask He *gives*. So says His Word again and again: "Ask and it shall be given you" (Mt 7:7), "every one that asketh receiveth" (Mt 7:8), "how much more shall your Father which is in heaven give good things to them that ask him" (Mt 7:11). But in the heart of that great chapter, the fourteenth of John, we come upon the greatest promise God has ever given to His praying children. Presuming, as we do in all that is said in these opening chapters concerning prayer, that the child of God is asking in His name, or according to His will, the wondrous statement is here twice made that not only as we pray does God give, but that as we pray God works.

God, the eternal God of the universe, stands, as it were, like an almighty servant and says, "if you, my child, will only *pray* I will *work*; if you will only be busy with *asking* I will see to the *doing*." Not only does He bestow at our cry, but He acts. Not only does our praying evoke His bounty, it sets in motion His omnipotence. Wherefore, as we enter into the secret chamber of prayer, nothing will so stir us to mighty intercession, nothing will so soon make us master-pleaders with God for a lost world, as to whisper to our own soul, again and again, this wonderful truth, "while I am praying God is really doing that which I am asking."

Thus to a child of God bowed in prayer that the gospel may be sent to the dark lands, though he may not see it, yet as he prays God baffles the powers of darkness; as he prays God moves the hearts of kings; as he prays God breaks down the barriers to evangelization; as he prays God loosens the bands of superstition; as he prays God opens up the pathways to forbidden lands; as he prays God unclasps the purses of His children; as he prays God raises up and thrusts forth the gospel messengers to the whitened harvests. As he is praying God is doing. This is explicitly asserted. "Search my word," says our Lord. "Find out clearly in it what My will is concerning the world. Pray according to that will. Then as you pray, 'Lord thrust forth laborers into the harvest,' I thrust them forth! As you pray, Lord break down the obstacles,' I break them down! As you pray, 'Lord stir men's hearts to give.' I stir them! Whatsoever ye *ask* in my name, I *do*."

Beloved, what a tremendous responsibility is ours! What a unique privilege! That all the power of an omnipotent God is ready and waiting to be put into triumphant, irresistible action at the prayer of one of His children! That the very hosts of heaven are marshalled against the powers of darkness at that importunate call of yours which is according to the will of God! He declares that all power in heaven and earth is His, and then, as it were, places Himself at our disposal and says, "Now my child *you pray* and *I* will *work;* you *ask* and *I* will *do*."

As an engineer might suffer a child to call forth power, not its own, by opening the throttle of his great machine, so God says to us weaklings, "all power is mine, but unto you it is given to call it forth by prayer." *If it be true, then, that God's omnipotence is placed at our disposal, we are as responsible for its exercise through prayer as though we possessed it ourselves.* Behold here the shame of an unevangelized world, of two thousand years delay, of our cowardice and faltering in the presence of difficulties. For though we have had no power to do, yet the mighty God, linking Himself with us as a real yoke-fellow and co-worker, has said, "If ye ask I will do."

It is a promise by an omnipotent Doer.

They who are charged with the erection of costly public or private buildings count it a rare privilege to have a great artist offer his services. They seek to employ the greatest architect, the most famous painter, the most skillful sculptor to do their work. But who is it here who offers to do for us, if we will only ask? It is no untried apprentice, no bungling worker accustomed to failure. It is God Himself. It is the mightiest doer in the universe who says "I will do, if you ask." Unrivalled wisdom, boundless skill, limitless power, infinite resources are His. Think a moment who it is that promises.

He who shrouded the land of Egypt in awful darkness; He who turned her streams of water to streams of blood; He who laid His hand upon her firstborn and filled her borders with mourning; He who broke the stubborn will of her impious king; He who led forth His people Israel, with mighty arm and outstretched hand; He who parted the great sea, and made the glassy walls of water to be bulwarks of safety to them, and swift avalanches of death to their pursuing foes; He who, when His children cried for water, sweetened the bitter wells to quench their thirst; He who, when they hungered sent them bread from heaven; He who, when they marched about Jericho in utter self-helplessness, leveled its towering walls by the word of His power; He who walked with His three children in the fierce, fiery furnace, yet kept them even

37

from the smell of scorching garments; He who stilled the tempest, walked on the seas, cast out devils, healed the living and raised the dead—it is this same mighty *Doer* who says He will do for me, if I ask! This omnipotence is the very same omnipotence whose doing is awaiting my praying!

Yea, the God who holds the sea in the hollow of His hand; the God who swings this ponderous globe of earth in its orbit more easily than you could swing a child's rubber ball; the God who marshals the stars and guides the planets in their blazing paths with undeviating accuracy; the God of Sinai, and of Horeb; the heaven-creating, devil-conquering, dead-raising God, it is this very God who says to you and to me, "If ye ask I will do."

It is a promise which shows how much more wonderful than our doing is His doing called forth by our asking.

You can at will close your eyes and, in vision, call up before you the men and women whom you love yet know to be lost. Friend after friend has wrought with and entreated them; you yourself would almost be willing to be anathema for them, if so be they might be saved. But all has been in vain. Suppose now there came some day a message from the Lord Jesus Christ promising that if you would but ask, He Himself would go to these unsaved ones and deal directly with them.

What an unheard of privilege would you count it to have Jesus Christ deal personally with a soul you loved! To have Jesus Christ work—not indeed in the body but in the Spirit—in your home, your church, your community; to have Jesus Christ give secret messages to your lost loved ones; to have Jesus Christ speak, woo, and win, as none else could; to have Jesus Christ with all His tact, wisdom, winsomeness, patience, gentleness, and compassion following on with unwearied zeal and tenderest love to bring back to God that soul for whom He had died; what a promise! And yet this is exactly what prayer will accomplish, for He explicitly says, "If ye *ask* I will *do*."

Think a moment of that unsaved loved one for whom all these years you have been doing. You have pleaded, argued, and expostulated in vain. You have preached Christ, you have tried to live Christ. You have exhausted every device and means that love, faith, or hope could conceive. Now that all your doing has failed how wondrous it would be into that life to bring His doing through your asking.

Hear Him speak: "My child *you* know not how to convict of sin, but *I*, who work as you pray, can bow down that soul in a very agony of conviction. *You* know not when to woo, and when to reprove, but *I*, who work as you ask, know just when to pour in the balm of love, and when to let fall the sharp, quick blow of needed judgment. *You* cannot follow a soul in daily, unbroken pursuit, for you are finite and must eat, rest, and sleep, but *I*, who do as you ask, follow that soul day and night, with sleepless vigilance, through every second of his existence. Now comforting, now troubling; now giving darkness, now light; now sending prosperity, now adversity; now using the knife, now the healing balm; chastening, troubling; bereaving, blessing; bending, breaking, making, yea, *I* can do all things needful to be done to bring that wanderer to himself and cause him to cry, 'I will arise and go unto my Father.'"

What a message, too, is this for God's children who, through years of pain and affliction as invalids and "shut-ins," have mourned because cut off from the active service in which others are busy for God. Beloved sufferers, be comforted. Blessed as is the ministry of *doing,* there is no higher, holier calling under heaven than that *asking* which calls forth *God's doing* in the lives of others. Your Master Jesus Christ, through every second of His eternal, heavenly life, is pouring out His soul in *unceasing asking* ("He ever liveth to make intercession," Heb 7:25).

What an honor that God should call you to that same

eternal ministry to which His great Son now unceasingly gives Himself! Covet no other if this be thine. To enter into a needy life with your own doing is indeed precious, but to have God enter it through your *asking,* is it not greater by so much as God's doing is greater than thine? Hear Him speak to you. "O child of mine, laid upon a bed of helplessness and suffering, cease to repine because thou can'st not busy thyself with thine own doing, as others. For I tell thee that as in the silence of the night watches thou dost cry unto me for a lost world, I am *doing* what of my will thou art *asking.* Wouldst thou not rather call forth mine omnipotent doing by thine asking if to this I have called thee, than even to be busy with thine own doing? For if thou shalt ask (according to my will) I will do."

And let your glad answer be, "Lord I rejoice. Though, shut within these four walls, I cannot touch men yet Thou who hast promised to do for me, wilt touch and quicken them if I but ask. Though I am all the day weary and helpless yet Thou, who hast promised to do for me, are in Thy doing tireless and omnipotent. Though I cannot raise a hand nor stir a foot yet Thou, who hast promised to do if I ask, wilt move heaven and earth to bless those for whom I pray. Though my human asking must soon end with my passing away, yet Thy mighty doing, called forth by my asking, will go on through all time, yea through eternity itself. Yea, Lord, since I can pray down Thy mighty doing into the lives I love, shall I longer mourn because I am shut out from my doing? What though I cannot do if Thou who dost work at my asking can do miracles? So Lord, though I can do nothing, help me to remember with new joy and hope thy blessed promise: 'If ye ask I will do.' "

It is a promise for our service.

Concerning those things that only God can do we naturally betake ourselves to prayer. For knowing that we

40

ourselves cannot do them, we find our hope only in that asking which brings God's doing. But let us remember, too, that our own personal service, in the things which we can do, needs also that asking which will bring God's doing into it. Do we realize that everything we do needs to be saturated with the spirit of prayer that God may be the real doer, the real worker in the things which we are busily doing? Yes, this is a mighty truth: "If ye ask I will do" applies to your own service as well as your intercession for others.

Have you ever toyed with the key of a telegraph instrument while the circuit was closed? If so, you have noted this fact. On that key you may write a complete message, from address to signature. Upon it every telegraphic character may be perfectly formed; every condition of expert operating may be fulfilled. But it matters not how skillful an operator you are, so long as the electric circuit is closed, all your efforts are simply sounding brass and clattering platinum. Not a single spark of electric life do you transmit; not a single message of good or ill, of bane or blessing is conveyed to the waiting listener at the other end of the line. Why? *Because the battery is not working.* And all your working is effort without result, activity without power. But now you open the little brass lever which connects your key to the battery hidden beneath the table. Immediately every letter you form thrills with life, every word you write flashes a living message into the mind and heart of the faraway receiver. Through your work, dead and mechanical in itself, the electric battery is now pouring forth its vital stream, flooding with life and power every deft motion of your flying fingers.

The lesson is plain. It is in spiritual telegraphy as in material. If the battery is not working the message is mere clatter. *We* may *do,* but if *God* is not doing through us then all our doing is naught. If we work in our own fleshly strength we will but effect fleshly results, for "whatsoever is born of the flesh *is* flesh." God alone is

41

spiritual life. God is the only begetter of life. Our highest function as servants is to be transmitters of the life of God to others. Our highest doing is that in which God is doing through us.

And how shall this be? Through prayer. Prayer connects you with the divine battery of life and power. Prayer puts you "in the Spirit," and "it is the Spirit that quickeneth." From the chamber of prayer you come forth to men with the unction, the subtle power, the thrill of God's own life upon you, and as you touch them in speech, deed, or prayer, "virtue goes forth from you," for then it is not you but God that worketh in you. As you keep asking, God keeps doing. When you grow prayerless your deeds grow powerless. Lead no meeting without *asking* that God may be the real leader through you; speak no message without *asking* that He may speak through you; begin no work without *asking* that God may work through you, for "If ye ask I will do."

THE SPIRIT-FILLED LIFE

He that believeth on me, as the scripture hath said, out of his belly shall flow rivers of living water. But this spake he of the Spirit, which they that believe on him should receive. JOHN 7:38-39

If, some summer day, you were tramping down a certain mountain pass, you would, by and by, come to one of the most famous of Swiss glaciers. In the perpendicular wall of that great glacier, summer sun and warm winds have hollowed out a great ice cavern. You enter the arch, and, as you stand in the fantastic cave, you are chilled through with its cold. Ice above you; ice before you; ice all about you; masses of ice; miles of ice. And now, as you gaze, there springs up at your feet a crystal stream of water from the very heart of the glacier, and begins its journey down the valley. You could almost step across it where it finds its birth. But, like the true Christian life, as it goes it grows, and a few miles down the valley, it is a strong, deep, leaping stream. The birds dip their bills into it, and, drinking, lift their heads to God as if in thanksgiving. The trees slip their roots down the bank and draw up its moisture. The lowing herds sink their nostrils in its pools and drink of its refreshing. By and by it enters a great lake, and seems lost. But it finds issue, and crossing central France, it takes a sudden turn and runs southward, and then, at its mouth, broad enough for fishermen to draw their seines, and for great ships to sail upon its bosom, it is at last lost in Europe's greatest inland sea. And this beautiful, sparkling river, with all its refreshing and blessing, springs from the frozen heart of a great Swiss glacier!

Have you ever looked up into the Lord's face and cried, "O, Christ, how cold my heart is! How cold when I study Thy blessed Book with all its wondrous words of life; how callous it seems in the sacred chamber of secret prayer; how icy as I look with such seeming unconcern upon the sin and suffering of the lost world; how frozen in its lack of love for the Christless millions of heathendom! O Christ, is there anything that will melt this iceberg heart of mine and cause a river of love and peace and power to flow forth from it to the world about me?" And Jesus Christ says, "There is. I have it." The God who can cause a river of refreshing to break forth from the frigid heart of an Alpine glacier can make a river of life burst forth from your cold heart. Are you a believer? Then listen. "Out of *your*"—do you heed it?—"out of *your* innermost being shall flow rivers of living water."

Let us be glad that Christ has made this truth so plain. Metaphors and similes are often hard to explain. One man has one interpretation, another man a different one. But here there is no chance for wrangling or disputings; none for difference of interpretation. The Holy Spirit interprets this passage Himself. For the Word of God says of this beautiful figure, "This spake He of *the Spirit* which they that believe on Him should receive." There is no room for doubt about it. God is talking about a river of spiritual blessing; about the river of His own life that He means shall flow from the heart and life of every child of His. And no power in earth has a right to cheat us of that blessed river of life. It is our birthright, and no man can keep us out of it if we fulfill the simple conditions Christ gives.

This river of life is the normal life of the Christian.

We recall a glorious morning drive under the sky of a southern spring day. The world seemed intoxicated with life. The tree roots were sucking life from the earth in which they were hid. The trunks were passing it upward to the branches. The branches were pouring it forth to the very tips of the swelling buds. The seeds buried in the ground were quickening with life. The day was humming with the drone and buzz of insect life. The very air you breathed made the pulsing blood leap and thrill with life. And the thought was borne home with power, "if God's normal plan for His physical world is one of such a-bounding, overflowing life, why should it not be the same for the spiritual life of His own children?" "Ah," you say, "but this river of the Spirit is the exceptional life. It is beyond the ordinary. It is not the normal life of the believer of today." Are we sure of that? What *is* the believer's normal life? Is the *usual* life of the Christian the normal life God has designed for him? Or, does it not rather reveal the shame of his shortcomings?

To know nothing of the power of God; to live a barren, fruitless life in the kingdom of God; to have no delight in the service of God: to be so allied with the world as hardly to be known as the children of God—is *this* the normal life of God's child? No, never. It may be the usual life—alas for that!—but it is never the normal life. It may be the one we are living. But it is an awful sag from the one Christ means us to live.

Would you look upon a picture of the normal life? Here it is. Mark it well. "And the multitude of them that believed were of one heart and of one soul . . . . and great grace was upon them all. And all that believed were together. . . . And they, continuing daily with one accord in the temple, and breaking bread from house to house, did eat their meat with gladness and singleness of heart, praising God and having favour with all the people. And the Lord added to the church daily such as should be saved" (Acts 4:32, 2:44, 46-47). Lives filled with grace and joy, love and unity, testimony and power, and favor both with men and God—these were the normal lives in those glad days. Yea, and God means these to be the normal lives yet. Verily, this life is not the exception in God's plan. It is the type. It is the worldly, powerless, fruitless Christian life which is abnormal, that is, away from the normal. The Spirit-filled life is God's own pattern in the mount: God's own perfect model for our lives. For God never has designed and never will endure any substitute for the individual, consecrated, Spirit-filled life, and any church which falls short of this high ideal will miss its high calling, however pretentious its claims, however elaborate its organization.

This river of life is in us who believe.

A belated ship had come in from sea. Her water barrels were exhausted. Her crew were perishing with thirst. By and by they sighted another vessel, and the cry went up from the perishing men, "Send us water; send us water." Back from the captain of the other ship came the strange reply: "Throw over your pails and draw." "But we want not this salt water to madden our thirst. We are famishing for life-giving water." Back again came the same strange reply: "Throw over your pails and draw." Once again with parched lips and burning throats, the now desperate crew called for water. And then came back the answer: "You are in the mouth of the Amazon. Throw over your pails and draw." And, sure enough, all unknown to themselves, they had sailed into the mouth of the Amazon, which is, at midriver, so wide as to be out of sight of land. And all the while they were thirsting, perishing, and crying for water, the sweet, fresh water of that great river was all about them. They needed only to draw, to drink, and find life.

Just so are men and women crying out to God for the Holy Spirit to come: pleading for a baptism of the Holy Spirit; waiting to receive the Holy Spirit. Yet, all the while, the Holy Spirit is here. For this river of life, this Spirit of the living God, becomes the possession of every one of His children upon belief in Jesus Christ for salvation. If there were no other test to prove this than Christ's own word here that would seem to be all-

sufficient. How clear and explicit it is. "He that believeth
... out of his belly shall flow." "But this spake he of
the Spirit, which they that believe on him should receive"
(Jn 7:38-39). No other condition named, none other
needed, but this simple one of faith in Him for salvation.
The faith which trusts Him then for salvation; and then
the faith which presses on to give the life to Him in
dedication; which commits all things to His keeping;
which draws day by day upon Him for His resurrection
life; which constantly leans upon and lives upon Him for
all things—it is this faith alone which the fuller, more
complete, and more all-sweeping it becomes brings to the
child of God an ever increasing, ever enriching knowledge
of the indwelling Spirit of God.

Of like import is our Lord's word to His disciples in
the fourteenth chapter of John. There He tells them that
the Father will send them "another Comforter." "For He
dwelleth with you and shall be in you" (Jn 14:17). That
word "another" is significant. There are two words for
it in the Greek. One means another of a different kind.
Interestingly enough, our English word "another" con-
tains this double meaning. For example: You go into a
hardware store to buy a penknife. You select one seemingly perfect. But when you come to use it you find it otherwise. The edge is dull. The steel is brittle and worthless.
The first strain you put upon the blade snaps it in two.
You go back to the merchant and say, "This knife does
not please me at all. I want another." You mean another
of a different kind. But, now suppose when you buy your
second knife you find it just right. The blade is keen as a
razor. The steel is of the finest quality. The handle is of a
beautiful pearl. You are delighted with your purchase.
You think of a friend to whom you would like to give
one like it. So you go back again to the merchant and say,
"I am delighted with this knife. Please give me another."
And now you mean another of the same kind, exactly
like the one you have just bought.

When the Lord Jesus was going away from His own

and said, "The Father will send you another Comforter," He used the Greek word which means "another of the same kind." That is, the very same as Himself. "The very same life you have seen flowing from Me; the very same the Father sent down from heaven with Me: the very same by which He has done His wondrous works through Me; that very same Holy Spirit shall be in you, even as He was not in the Old Testament saints. He was *with* them; but he shall be *in* you." And so with all reverence, yet with all joy and gladness of heart may we say that the very same Holy Spirit who dwelt in the Lord Jesus Christ, the Son of God, is dwelling in us, God's children. Let us believe upon His word, that He is so indwelling in all of us who are believers in Him, and just waiting for a chance to live out His life in all its fullness through us.

And so we pass naturally to our next thought, that

This river of life will fill us as we yield.

The stream of life and power from God runs along the riverbed of the will of God. Wherefore the man or woman who is most fully in the will of God must most fully know the life and fullness of God. The one Man who had the Spirit "without measure" was He who at the beginning said to God, "Lo, I came to do Thy will." In other words, self-will is a dyke; the yielded will is a channel. The dyke of self-will keeps out the fullness of God's life. But the channel of the yielded will furnishes an avenue for its outflow. Why does the harp breathe forth its ravishing strains under the hand of the master-harper? Because it is *yielded* to him. Why is the molten bronze filled with every outline of the beauty of the mold? Because it is *yielded* to it. Why does the great ship plough her way through storm and surge to her destined haven? Because she is *yielded* to the will and touch of the helmsman. If the harp, and the bronze, and the ship each had a will of its own it could hinder the master's highest purpose for it. You *do* have such a will. And you *can* resist God. Therefore you must yield the life to Him, if so be that He may fill it. And that fuller life will come. It may not be in a flash. It may come by degrees. But as you yield your life by one definite act, and then, day by day, learn to live out that act in a life of yieldedness and ministry, God's river of life will surely and steadily manifest itself from your innermost being.

This river of life will flow forth from us as we serve.

That was a sweet prayer of a young Christian girl: "Lord, fill me to overflowing. I cannot hold much. But I can overflow a great deal." And she was right. For with many the desire concerning the Holy Spirit is to hold, and to enjoy. Whereas with God it is to give, and to overflow to others. For we see the Spirit of God here pictured as a great, life-giving river. But every river needs an outlet. When it has none it ceases to be a river, and becomes only a stagnant pool. The river of the Spirit is subject to the same great river-law. It seeks an outlet for the divine outflow of life and love in everyday, practical ministry to others. It begins its flow as soon as it finds a channel. And it keeps it up so long as we remain such. Jesus does not say "In his belly shall *stay*" but "*out* of his belly shall *flow*" these living streams. That is one purpose for which rivers exist—to flow. Cut off their outlet, and you stop the flow.

Here is an open secret for us all. The man or woman who will offer the Spirit-river this simple outlet of humble, willing service will know His steady overflow. People plunge the probe of self-examination into their inner selves, seeking all sorts of inward, subjective causes for their failure of spiritual life and experience. Ordinarily the reason for that failure is amazingly simple, and near at hand. Is the life selfish and self-centered? Is it failing in daily, practical ministry to others? And would you know the remedy? It is this. Do not try to shut up the Spirit in a stagnant pool of selfishness. Let Him have His river-way of flow through outlet—the outlet of loving, practical service to others. Try this. Then all your spiritual moods and morbidness will disappear in the daily, joyful consciousness of His steady outflow through the channel of service.

This river of life may flow forth from us unconsciously.

I was in a great city, teaching. A difficult question of guidance had arisen. Day after day I had prayed about it. But the perplexity seemed only to increase. At last I came to the danger point of anxiety, so earnestly had light been sought and found not. And then this happened. One morning before the dawn I suddenly awakened from sleep. The first consciousness that came in the darkness was that a heavy wagon was rumbling past the window, in the street outside. The next was that someone on the wagon—presumably its driver—was whistling a tune. And the next vivid impression was of the tune he was whistling. It was

> Trust and obey,
> For there's no other way
> To be happy in Jesus,
> But to trust and obey.

Like a flash in darkness came the thought as from the Lord, "Why, my child, this is all I expect of you. Simply act upon the light as best you see it, and trust Me to lead you. There is nothing you need but to trust and obey." At once I saw I had been unduly anxious about the guidance, and that this was the exact message I needed in this time of perplexity and uncertainty. Light flooded my pathway. Perplexity made way for peace. The problem was solved. The rumble of the dray wheels died away in the distance. The song of the whistler ceased. But a message had gone straight home to my heart more wondrous than any sermon ever heard. I do not know whether the unseen whistler was a child of God. But I believe it. And out from his innermost being was flowing that river of life which brought into the life of another child of God such a touch of life, and light, and refreshing as he who passed on into the darkness never knew or dreamed.

"O Lord," said one of His saints, "I thank Thee that Thou hast forgotten all the sins I remember, yet dost remember all the good deeds I have forgotten." That is true. And out from our lives, all unconscious to us, may flow a stream of influence and blessing of which we may in no wise be conscious. But He does not forget it. And it shall all be revealed in the day of manifestation to our unspeakable joy, and His eternal glory.

> This learned I from the shadow of a tree,
>   Which to and fro swayed on a garden wall
>   Our shadow-selves, our influence, may fall
> Where we can never be.

"And he shewed me a pure river of water of life . . . proceeding out of the throne of God" (Rev 22:1).

"This Jesus . . . having received of the Father the promise of the Holy Ghost . . . hath shed forth this, which ye now see" (Ac 2:32-33).

Wonderful river of life! It proceedeth from the very throne of the Father. It was received by the Son from the Father. It is shed forth by the Son upon us other children of the Father. And now as we believe—and yield—and serve, it will abide—fill—and flow forth from us to the sinning, suffering, dying world here below which so sorely needs the touch of His divine life through us, His Spirit-indwelt children.

THE BLESSING OF DOING

If ye know these things, blessed are ye if ye do them.
JOHN 13:17, ASV

One of the fondest memories of your boyhood days is that of the old swimming hole. Hidden away in the cool depths of the woods, it was your favorite boyish resort. Especially do you recall one hot summer day when you betook yourself to it for a cool swim. The day was stifing. Your body was throbbing and feverish with the great heat. You were soon ready for the plunge. You raised your hands above your head. And then you hesitated. You dipped your foot into the water. You touched it with the tip of your fingers. You sprinkled a bit of it upon your heated body. But still you dallied and delayed. And all the while you postponed your plunge there came no physical blessing to your body. But by and by your indecision ended. You raised your hands above your head. You backed off and took a little run. And then came the plunge. And to this very day you remember the cool, tingling, refreshing sense of physical blessing that suffused your tired, overheated body, and set it all aglow and atingle with the sheer sense of physical joy. So long as you dallied and hesitated there came no manifestation of physical blessing. But as soon as you plunged, it was there. It was the blessing of doing.

That is a homespun illustration of our Lord's luminous statement, "If ye know these things, blessed are ye if ye do them." What does he mean by this teaching? Simply this. There are some truths which we need only to *believe* in order to have the blessing of them. But there are others which need to be *obeyed* ere that blessing comes. Merely to know them is not enough. We must also do

52

them. Such are all of Christ's commands. The blessing from them comes in the doing of them. And it is only as we obey them that the rich blessing of them becomes ours.

The Greatest Blessing

Suppose some day I meet you upon the street. Your face is radiant. Your voice is vibrant with feeling. Your whole attitude shows the stress of a great emotion. I say to you, "You must have had a great blessing today somewhere." Then you tell we what has just happened. As you suddenly turned the corner of a street you came upon your beloved mother. You did not dream she was within a hundred miles of the city. But all unexpectedly you came face to face with her dear self and it has filled your heart with unbounded joy and blessing. Ah, I see what your blessing is. It is the manifested personal presence of one most dearly beloved to yourself. There could be no greater blessing than this. But that which is true in the sphere of the affections is also true in the spiritual life. The greatest possible blessing of our spiritual beings is the personal manifestation of Jesus Christ in our innermost hearts. When Jacob ended his all night struggle against the unseen God the narrative tells us "He blessed him there." Jacob showed what the heart of that blessing was by the name which he gave to the place. He called it *Peniel,* which means "the face of God." "For," said he, "I have seen God face to face." With Jacob, as with all of God's children, blessing was the personal revelation of God to his own soul.

Our Lord beautifully sets forth this truth in John 13:17. There He says that if we know His commandments, blessed are we if we do them. Now link this with John 14:21. There He says that if we keep (or do) His commandments He will manifest Himself to us. Thus the supreme and precious blessing of the personal manifestation of Jesus Christ's presence in our hearts is conditioned upon our doing His will. How mysterious and how incomprehensible do we make this conscious presence of Christ in our hearts to be! Yet how simple, clear, and comprehensible does our Lord make it in a statement so luminous that a child could understand it. Instead of being a mystical, difficult truth it is one which lies right upon the surface in the full sunshine of His clear and beautiful teaching. Let us consider some of the commandments which bring to us the joy of the Christ-consciousness and which we are daily trampling upon, without realizing that by so doing we cloud the manifestation of that precious presence which is the greatest conscious spiritual blessing of the soul.

The Blessing of Believing

A young Southern lad was brought up under the tutelage of an old Negro "uncle." The strong affection common in such cases sprang up between them. All through his boyhood days·the old man cared tenderly and affectionately for the young lad. Uncle Charley could not read but his young master read *Pilgrim's Progress* to him. The old man led the boy to the Lord. By and by the latter went off to enter college. The years rolled on. In due course he entered the seminary to prepare himself for the Gospel ministry, and went out to his lifework. One day came from home to him the message that Uncle Charley was dying and was longing to see his young master. Dropping everything the latter hastened to the side of his beloved old friend, eager to render any ministry he could in his last hours. "Jim, read my text for me," said the dying man. The young minister slowly and reverently read John 3:16, the picture of God's wondrous love for lost men. "Jim, sign my name to that text," said old Uncle Charley. And the young minister wrote his name, and made his mark as they were wont to do in the old slavery days for those who could not write. As he did so, the dying slave said, "Let me touch the pen."

The slave chose not to leave the plantation after emancipation, and had been deeded a little cabin and an acre of land. He had "made his mark" when the contract was drawn up. And the young minister suffered the old man to touch the tip of the penholder with his finger as the mark was made. Presently the old man grew delirious. In his delirium they heard him say, "Aunt Dinah said that I must go through great tribulation to be saved. And Uncle Rastus said that I must be baptized to be saved. But Jim says I only have to believe on the Lord Jesus Christ, and I've signed the Book to show that I do."

Behold the blessing of believing! Through it comes the blessing of salvation. Not that a man can do anything to save himself. No work, no merit, no effort of his own can save him. Salvation is all of grace. But it is "by grace *through* faith." Until the command to believe in Jesus Christ is obeyed the grace of God in salvation can never be known. Until man obeys that command he literally "makes void the grace of God," so far as it concerns his own salvation. Thus the blessing of salvation, while it is wholly of God in Christ Jesus, is also the blessing of believing. "Blessed are they," said Christ to Thomas, "that have not seen and yet have believed" (Jn 20:29).

A Christian worker was trying to lead a young man to accept the grace of God in Christ by faith alone. The young man suddenly turned upon him and said, "I will never believe until I have an experience." The Christian worker flashed back, "You will never have an experience until you believe." And he was right. The manifestation of Jesus Christ in salvation comes to the man who obeys His command to believe. Here, as elsewhere, it is, "If ye keep my commandments I will manifest myself unto you" (Jn 14:23). Not only is this true of salvation but also for the saved there is

The Blessing of Trusting

You will recall that when God sent Moses into Egypt

55

He told him to tell the people that it was the I AM who sent him. But do you notice that Christ also calls Himself I AM? That is, Christ's presence is an eternally continued present. Even when He came to promise His presence to His disciples as He gave them the last commission, with almost 2,000 years of that presence before them, He said not, "Lo, I will be with you alway," but "Lo, I *am* with you alway." And so because His life was an ever continuous today He warned them earnestly, as recorded in Matthew 6, against anxious thought for the morrow. And it was the trust in Him as the I AM of today that was to keep them from the anxious care of tomorrow. So the believer who steps out of this trust of the today, steps out from the conscious presence of Him who is the I AM. The secret of abiding peace in Christ is to learn this great lesson of living in today: "Build a little fence of trust around today; Fill the space with loving deeds, And therein stay."

It is the hedging of today with this little fence of trust and staying therein that is one of the profound secrets of continuous peace in Christ in the Christian life. It is the violation of this profound and simple secret of faith that is responsible for the oft-repeated recurrence of the troubled heart in our lives, against which Christ so earnestly warns us. Christ never projected Himself into the tomorrow of anxious care as we do. He never lived that way when He was upon earth. Neither will He live that way in us. Therefore we are bound to dim and mar the consciousness of His presence whenever we step out of the charmed circle of today's trust into the gloom of tomorrow's anxiety. "Thou wilt keep him in perfect peace because he trusteth in thee." Trust is the inexorable condition of the believer's peace in Christ Jesus. And the inevitable result of unfaith is anxiety. Andrew Murray has beautifully stated it. "The beginning of anxiety is the end of faith. And the beginning of faith is the end of anxiety." Nor will we ever know victory over anxiety until we begin to treat it as sin. For such it is.

It is deep-seated distrust of the tender care of a Father who assures us again and again that even the falling sparrow is in His tender love and care. Suffering we may know, and sorrow we may know and have the Lord's conscious presence with us in it all. But anxiety is a demon from the pit; born of distrust; and nurtured in our soul at the costliest price we can possibly pay for it: the abiding peace of Jesus Christ to those who trust Him. Tear the mask from the face of anxiety and back of it you will always find the scowling visage of unfaith. "O ye of little faith," is the sore spot upon which Jesus Christ most often placed His finger of love. Let us be faithful enough to our own spiritual selves to face this destroyer of our peace as a sin against God. When trust becomes enshrined in our hearts, anxiety will become a foe under our feet. No so-called venial sin is more destructive in its ravages upon our spiritual lives than this one of anxious care. It falls like a deadly blight upon everything within its reach, and blackens the beautiful flower of faith wherever it touches it. And one of the most sobering phases of its deadly work is this. In throttling faith, anxiety chokes the very channel through which God is seeking to pour in His peace and power.

You recall that story of one of Cromwell's officers who was given to this sin of anxious care. One day his godly servant who knew how to live in the today and leave the tomorrow to the care of His Lord said to his worrisome master, "Master, the Lord ran this world before you came into it," to which his master quickly assented. "You expect Him to run it after you leave it, do you not?" Again the master nodded assent. "Then how would it do to let Him run it while you are in it?" It would make a vast difference in our harrassed, worried lives if we decided to trust Him to run this world while we are in it! He is going to do it anyhow and we might as well live in the quiet rest of faith as in the feverish torment of anxiety.

Henry Gibbud was a mission worker in the city of New York. He spent his life in work among the slums of that great city. He was a man of great devotion and wonderful power in prayer. On one occasion he had been working all night in the slums of the great city. Tired and sleepy at the end of his toil, he made his way in the dark of the morning to the Brooklyn ferry dock. He put his hand in his pocket to pay his fare homeward on the ferry boat. To his dismay he discovered that he did not have even the three cents needful to pay his fare. His heart sank in deepest discouragement. He closed his eyes and began to pray. "Lord I have been toiling all night in thy service, trying to bring lost men and women to Jesus Christ. I am hungry, tired, and sleepy. I want to get home to my beloved wife, and have not even the three cents needful for my fare. You have promised to supply all my needs. Will you not help me?" As he closed his earnest prayer, he opened his eyes. They fell upon something shining in the dust at his feet. He reached down and picked up the glittering object. It was a fifty-cent piece. He paid his fare and went on his way homeward rejoicing. What was the joy that flooded his heart? It was Jesus Christ's fulfillment of His promise. "If ye keep my commandments, I will manifest myself." Henry Gibbud had kept His commandment to pray in time of need. And Christ had wonderfully fulfilled the promise of His revealed person.

Men talk much of the philosophy of prayer; of the mystery of prayer; and of the reflex influence of prayer on the life. But the greatest truth the Christian man needs to know about prayer is the necessity of praying. The blessing of prayer is the blessing of doing. It comes not as we philosophize about prayer but as we pray. Samuel said to the children of Israel, "God forbid that I should sin against God in ceasing to pray for you." The greatest prayer disaster in any believer's life is the ceasing to pray. "If ye know this thing, blessed are ye if do it," is intensely true of the command to pray.

The Blessing of Choosing

I was standing on the top of a high city building in the early dawn of an autumn day. The city was lost in the gray and the gloom of an enveloping fog. You could not see a hundred feet into its depths. Presently I turned my head upward. Instantly the whole scene changed. Great patches of blue were breaking through the heavy fog. The white clouds were grouping themselves to begin their day's journey across the face of the sky. The rising sun was tipping their fleecy summits with the glory of the coming day. It was mine to choose which of these scenes should fill my innermost being. When I turned my face downward, I was filled with the gray and the gloom of the dismal fog. When I turned it upward, I was filled with the glory and the splendor of the coming day. Whichever I opened to filled me. If I knew this fact, blessed was I when I acted upon it. I had something to do with the fullness, whether it should be a fullness of gloom or a fullness of glory.

Is not this what Paul means when he says, "Be not drunk with wine . . . but be filled with the Spirit" (Eph 5:18).

Clearly he is teaching this. Your life is being lived in a twofold environment. On the one hand are the world, the flesh, the devil. On the other are Christ, the things of the Spirit, and the things of the heavenlies. You may open to the things of the flesh, as for example to wine drinking, gluttony, and other lusts of the flesh. Or you may choose to open to the Word, Christ, communion, prayer, service, and the other blessed things of the Spirit. It is yours to choose. Whichever you open your heart and members to will fill you. So that while fullness is of God and is His gift, it is also, in a profound sense, your own choice which determines whether you will be filled with the things of the Spirit, or those of the flesh. The tragedy of the unsaved life is that light has come into the world and men love, that is they choose, darkness rather than light. And the tragedy of the worldly Christian's life is that while the Spirit is here with His fullness of life, and the flesh is also here, he chooses the things of the flesh rather than those of God. Through the one comes the manifestation of the world; through the other that of Jesus Christ.

The Blessing of Cleansing

You remember the story of the heathen idol, Dagon. The Philistines placed Dagon in the same temple with the Ark of the Covenant which represented the presence of God. On the second morning, Dagon was found lying face downward, decapitated, and with the palms of his hands cut off, leaving only a mutilated torso in the presence of the Ark of God. The lesson is sharp and clear. There is no fellowship between the Spirit of Christ and the flesh. If Christ manifests Himself to His children who keep His commandments, then of necessity that manifestation is dimmed and veiled by the failure to cleanse ourselves from the sins of the flesh. "Let us cleanse ourselves from all filthiness of the flesh and spirit" (2 Co 7:1): we are too careless and too heedless about this searching command to cleanse ourselves from all filthiness of the flesh. The blessing of this cleansing is the blessing of a deeper, richer manifestation of the presence of Christ than we could possibly have if we endure tamely the presence and practice of the sins of the flesh. Whoso endures unchallenged, unpurged the practice of a known sin in his life and walk pays the costly price of a quenched manifestation of the presence of Jesus Christ at that particular point. Myriads of Christians fail to see this, and are suffering untold loss because of it.

I had a beloved Christian friend. He knew the Lord in a deep, rich way. But he was a long-standing victim to the tobacco habit. Frequently the Spirit had convicted him for a separation from the habit. But the matter seemed to him to be trivial and the obedience correspondingly so. One day he was walking alone in a long covered bridge. The old issue came up. He fought the battle to a finish and settled it by throwing away his tobacco. He came out of the bridge with a radiant face and a heart full of the manifestation of the Lord. He testified afterward that this seemingly trifling act of obedience had brought into his heart one of the greatest spiritual blessings of his life. The Lord had simply proven the truth of His words that He would manifest Himself to His children who walked in the pathway of His will however trivial the issue seemed to be to them. The issue which God raises with us in our secret soul may seem to be a trifle. But disobedience itself is no trifling thing. It lost Saul his kingdom. It will lose us something of the surpassingness of the knowledge of Christ in our hearts.

The Blessing of Yielding

A great London preacher was discoursing on that beautiful text in 2 Chronicles 29:27:

"When the burnt-offering began, the song of the Lord began also." He called attention to the fact that in the temple ritual the song of the Lord was not permitted to rise until the burnt offering had been laid upon the altar. He went on to show the precious truth that it was only when the life of the believer was laid upon the altar of consecration to Jesus Christ that the fullest joy of the Lord filled his heart and rose up in thanksgiving and praise to God. The next morning the great preacher went downtown to the railroad station to take a train out of the city. As he stepped upon the station platform he was greeted by a grimy-faced railroad porter with this striking sentence, "Mr. Brown, I live in the country where the music is." Archibald Brown looked upon the railroad porter in amazement, utterly failing to grasp the meaning of

this sentence. Recovering himself from his astonishment, he said, "I do not understand you, my dear man." Then the porter smiled again and said, "Mr. Brown, I was in your church service last night. I heard you preach upon that beautiful text which says that the song of the Lord was not allowed to rise in the Temple until the burnt offering had been laid upon the altar. Mr. Brown, I want to say that I know all about that, for I live in the country where the music is." And then the humble porter began and told the great preacher a story of the power, peace, and wondrous blessing which had overflowed into his life when he laid it in sacrifice at Jesus Christ's feet, a story which thrilled the great messenger of God from head to foot with the beauty, simplicity, and certainty with which God had met the offered sacrifice of the porter's life, and had caused him from that time forward to live in the country where the music is.

Reader, do you live in the country where the music is? And do you realize that the richest spiritual music of the heart, the song of the Lord in its fullness, only rises after the burnt offering has been laid upon His altar? The blessing of the manifestation of Jesus Christ in our innermost heart is all of grace. Yet it is also the blessing of doing, and God is waiting for that yielding on your part in order that He may fulfill His promise of manifestation to them who keep His commandment: "Yield yourselves unto God" (Ro 6:13). "Abraham, because thou hast done this thing, I will bless thee," said the Lord to His great servant. But what was this thing of which He spoke? It was the yielding up of His all to God in the person of his beloved son, Isaac. And when he yielded there came a rich blessing which God explained by saying, "Because thou hast done this thing." Do this thing and Jesus Christ will make true to you the promise of His manifestation to all them who obey His commandments.

HOLY GROUND

Put off thy shoes from off thy feet, for the place whereon thou standest is holy ground. EXODUS 3:5

Plymouth Rock and Independence Hall are holy ground to every patriotic American heart. Gettysburg, Antietam, and Fredericksburg are holy ground to every man of the North and man of the South who walks over those dramatic spots. The battlefields of France are holy ground to countless mothers, whose hearts turn tenderly to the cross-marked graves where the bodies of their precious boys sleep amid the hush and beauty of green fields and flowers. But do we realize this word of God to Moses that "the place whereon thou standest is holy ground"? That the daily, prosaic, seemingly humdrum round of our everyday life and toil is holy ground if we would only see it as God sees it and accept it from His hand, as the holy place where He is ready to work out His great purpose for our humble lives?

The place whereon thou standest is the holy ground of consecration.

Most of us believe that God needs consecrated men in the ministry, in the foreign mission fields, and in all forms of Christian work. But how many of us realize that the place whereon we stand in our daily, work-a-day life is holy ground, and that there is no limit to the blessedness and power with which God will use consecrated bankers, lawyers, physicians, clerks, mechanics, and other Christian laymen who give themselves to Him in consecration, in the holy ground of everyday life.

I was chatting one day with a dear Christian friend who said to me, "Have you ever heard about Nat's sandpile?" When I answered in the negative he told me this story. Nat was a beloved friend of ours. He was a building contractor. It so happened that in his native city down by the riverbank was a huge sandpile. To every one else but Nat it was merely an unsightly, worthless sandpile. But Nat had a vision about this sandpile. He saw that every truckload he sold would bring him a dollar. And when the sandpile was gone the leveled ground would make a fine site for a business block. So Nat bought the sandpile. When the news got abroad, many of his friends were smiling at the idea of his buying a worthless sandpile. But soon Nat's vision began to come true. Week after week he sold sand and leveled off the ground. By and by the sand was all sold; the ground was leveled off; a handsome business block was built on the site. Before the year was over, a good part of the wholesale trade of the city had moved into that block, and soon after he sold out making thousands of dollars by the operation.

Friend, you life may be obscure, untalented, and as worthless in your sight as that sandpile. But if you will treat the place in everyday life whereon you stand as holy ground, and give that life to God in consecration, God will make of it a beautiful structure enduring for His glory through all time and eternity.

The place whereon thou standest is the holy ground of God's call.

Most of us, when we picture God's call, think of something dramatic, revolutionary, and startling. The scene on the road to Damascus at once comes up. We see the great light in the sky; we hear the voice from heaven; we picture the revolutionizing effect of it all upon the great apostle to the Gentiles. But we forget the great number of men to whom God's call came when they stood upon the holy ground of their everyday life and service. God's call came to Samuel as he ministered in the daily round of the temple; it came to David in the sheepfold; it came to Moses after forty years in the back of the desert; it came to some of the disciples as they were mending and casting their nets. In all these cases the call came to them as they stood upon the holy ground of their daily duties.

There comes back to me an experience of my early manhood days. My health was utterly broken. All my own plans were crushed. As yet I had found none of God's. One day I was sitting at my table studying the Word of God. A great blessing came into my heart. It was glowing with joy and with the desire to give the same message to others. I leaned back in my chair and prayed, "Oh God, if you would only give me a chance to give this to others as you have given it to me." I arose from my chair and walked down stairs. My sister handed me my morning mail. The first letter I opened was from the secretary of a Young Men's Christian Association across the river from the little town in eastern Pennsylvania where I lived. It ran like this. "Dear Brother, Last night we decided to start a Bible class. We arose from our knees, after a half hour's prayer, impressed that you were the man we needed. Will you come over and teach this class for us?" It seemed but a small thing, but it looked to me like God's holy ground of service. That night I went and taught a Bible class of five big-hearted railroad men. God gave great blessing to my own soul, and seemed to help these dear men. I taught that Bible class as faithfully as I knew for a period of three years. Then came another class, and another. At the end of three years I was teaching ten Bible classes, and had found my lifework. The place of daily service whereon I had been standing proved to be holy ground, and I had found the joy of God's will for my life.

Let us then heed this great truth that God's call always has come, and always will come, to men who are standing on the holy ground of everyday, faithful service. If He wants us elsewhere, He will make it plain. But until He does so, stay where you are and count it holy ground whereon thou standest.

The place whereon thou standest is the holy ground of patience.

The literal meaning of the verb "to be patient" is "to stay under." It is a striking word picture. We sing:

> Have Thine own way, Lord,
>   Have Thine own way;
> Thou art the potter,
>   I am the clay.

But when the potter puts his hand on the clay, the clay proceeds to get out from under the potter's wheel instead of staying under the same. To stay under all that God permits to come upon you, whether of suffering, tribulation, or affliction while He works out His purpose of Christlikeness in you, that makes the place whereon thou standest to be the holy ground of patience.

How true this was of Moses. There in that barren, lonely spot, under the fiery rays of a desert sun, day after day, year after year, God kept His great servant in the place of patience. That is he "stayed under" the hand of God amid all the monotony, desolation, and isolation of those forty years of tremendous test and trial. Forty years of service. A year of patience for every year of leadership! And out of it the hotheaded, hasty young Egyptian killer came forth an iron-willed, stedfast, tenderhearted, marvelous leader with the very patience of God Himself. For none other would have sufficed to lead this raw, undisciplined, rebellious, unbelieving, idolatrous host of Israelites through all those weary years of wandering which their own sinfulness had brought upon them, yet which he shared with them as though he himself were responsible with them for the tragedy of it all.

Much of our prayer life consists in beseeching God to surround us with a new set of circumstances. Instead of that we should pray for grace to stay under the present circumstances while He works out in us His purpose of Christlikeness. God does not need a new set of circumstances to make you Christlike. All He needs is for you to "stay under the old set with which He has environed your life. I question if there is any Christian reading these lines who needs a change of circumstances as much as he needs that Christlike change in himself which God is seeking to work out as he stays under his present conditions.

A young man came into my room one day for a conference. He said he had been praying earnestly to God to make an important change in his environment, but God had failed to do so. So his faith had been much shaken. I suggested that God might have a purpose in keeping him where he was, and that it might be well to submit it all to Him and stay under His hand while He worked out His great purpose. We got down upon our knees together and I prayed that he might make such a committal. I waited a moment to hear it, but when I looked up he was standing with his hand upon the door knob ready to go out. He had no intention nor desire to stay under God's hand, but was getting ready to get out. We pray to God to change our environment, but when God puts His hand upon us to change us, instead of staying under that hand we reach for the door to get out. Of course if God Himself changes our circumstances it is different. But until He does so, it is well for us to stay under our present environment, realizing that the place whereon we stand is the holy ground of patience for us.

The place whereon thou standest is the holy ground of suffering.

"For He that hath suffered in the flesh hath ceased from sin; that he no longer should live the rest of his time in the flesh to the lusts of men, but to the will of God" (1 Pe 4:1-2).

This is a striking text. It clearly teaches that the children of God, through their experiences of suffering, pass from doing the lusts of the flesh into the blessed place of living in the will of God. Thus the place of suffering where we stand becomes the holy ground of submission to the will of God. This may not seem true to us while we are passing through it. But as the years go by, and we see how our lives have been deepened and enriched through suffering, we begin to realize what holy ground this place of suffering is whereon we stand.

I once heard a dear Christian man tell this story. He had a beloved son. He was one of those rare personalities, winsome, lovable, and outstanding in the beauty and strength of his character. The young man was taken to a hospital for an operation. He came through all right and seemed to be convalescing rapidly. His father had a long and important railroad journey to take, but hesitated to leave his sick boy. The latter, however, wished him to go, telling him that it was all right, and as the father leaned over him to say good-by, the lad kissed him and bade him God speed. Three or four days brought the father back from the long journey. He hastened to the first telephone booth, picked up the phone, and inquired at the hospital how his boy was. The answer came back like a bolt from a clear sky, "He is dead." A spasm of pain swept over the father's face as he uttered these words, and uncovered the agony of his soul after a lapse of six years. But a new light was in his eye, and a new joy in his voice as he told me how he had found the blessed will of God for his life, and what unspeakable joy he was finding in doing that precious will. The suffering had done its work. It was the holy ground of God's will for him.

Back to me comes the recollection of years of suffering in my own life. I was called home from college by the death of my father. There fell upon me the care of a paralyzed mother, seven children, and thousands of dollars of debt. It was the place of loving duty, and I unhesitatingly stepped into it. But what years of suffering they were! I was only a boy and the burden was great. Year after year passed by, and how dark they were as I look back over them now. At last the awful debts were paid; my brother was a successful young business man; my sisters were happily married; and my beloved mother was "absent from the body and present with the Lord." I myself was physically crushed. The path of suffering had been a thorny one, and the way seemed hard and long. Now that the years have fled, and "I trace the rainbow through the rain," those years of suffering have proved to be the holiest ground upon which my feet have ever trodden. For in them, and because of them, I passed out from the will of the flesh concerning my own life into the precious place of the will of God. I learned obedience through the things which I had suffered. All that I passed through I needed, nor would I recall one day of it now, as I think of the unspeakable blessing it has brought to my life.

What do you think was the holiest ground upon which the feet of our blessed Lord trod after His resurrection glory came to him? I am sure it was under the gnarled olive trees of Gethsemane where he sweated blood in coming into the perfect will of God; and the hill of Calvary, where He poured out the crimson tide of His life for you and me when "He loved us and gave Himself for us." And when you and I come back in our glorified bodies to revisit these earthly scenes, I am sure the holiest ground upon which our feet shall tread will be the places where we suffered.

The place whereon thou standest is the holy ground of service.

In my college days there was a boy in the class above me whom we called Tom. He was quiet and somewhat reserved, but was able, scholarly, and withal popular among the boys. We all thought he would make good when he went out into the world. Graduation day came and with it the breaking of college ties and the parting of college friends. Thirty-five years rolled by. Then one day I heard that our old college mate, whose full name was Thomas Woodrow Wilson, was to speak in this city. I went down to the great hall to hear him. There I found a splendid audience of four thousand Christian men gathered to hear his message upon a great moral and religious theme. It was a magnificent address and captivated his audience by its eloquence and literary finish. At its close I went up and greeted him, and we had a pleasant chat about the old college days. He went back to the White House, and I wended my way down to a little two-room office on the tenth floor of a city skyscraper. I sat there thinking of my old college friend. He was at the zenith of his fame. The eyes not only of the country, but of all the world were centered upon him. My own life was quiet, obscure, hidden away in a little corner whence I was sending out over the world simple devotional messages from the Lord. Yet do you know, that as I looked into my own heart, I could not find one atom of envy toward my distinguished fellow collegian, nor of covetousness for his high position. Do you ask why? Simply because I had found the humble place in which my lot was cast to be God's holy ground of service, and that was the joy of all life to me. Cherish in your thoughts and incarnate in your life this wonderful sentence of Hudson Taylor:

> Be God's man;
> In God's place;
> Doing God's work;
> In God's way.

The place whereon thou standest is the holy ground of soul-winning.

We say there are yet four months to the harvest. We postpone our soul-winning to some indefinite future, or some time of special services in our churches. But Christ says the fields are white to the harvest. He points us to the immediate present, right at our hand. He calls upon us to buy up the opportunity, to redeem the time which is every day at our doors. "Today" is the ever present

70

"now" of soul-winning and is the only holy ground upon which our feet do stand.

One night in a Canadian town a young man arose in a city mission and gave this remarkable testimony. He said he was a passenger on the ill-fated Titanic when that great ship went down. He was thrown into the water in the darkness and managed to scramble to a piece of wreckage, where he held fast. By and by a man drifted near to him who was holding to a similar bit of wreckage. As he came near he called across the water to the other man, "Young man, are you saved?" The young man replied, "No, sir." Back came the words, "Believe on the Lord Jesus Christ, and thou shalt be saved." Then the speaker drifted away into the darkness. By and by through some strange happening, not chance, the stranger drifted within hailing distance of the young man, and called out over the water again, "Young man, are you saved now?" Again the young man replied, "No, sir." Again the voice came back, "Believe on the Lord Jesus Christ, and thou shalt be saved." Then a wave swept over the speaker. It broke his grasp, and he went down to death in a watery grave. "And then," said the young man, "with two miles of sea underneath me, I believed on the Lord Jesus Christ and was saved." Then, with intense earnestness, the young man added this closing sentence, "I'm John Harper's last convert."

Truly that was making the last moments of life the holy ground of soul-winning. For this momentous work of soul-winning there is no other time but now; there is no other holy ground but the present, upon which our feet can stand.

"Put off thy shoes from off thy feet."

What does that mean? Simply this. Cease treating the daily round of your life as a common thing. It is holy ground. Every day is aflame with the presence of God, even though your blinded eyes fail to recognize it. Every

71

golden hour is a tiny square in the mosaic of God's beautiful pattern for your life. Every opportunity is a holy chance to win a soul from the kingdom of darkness into the kingdom of the Son of His love. Every distress and necessity is but a new lesson in the matchless school of patience, teaching you how to "stay under" the hand of the skilled Potter who is fashioning you as a vessel of honor and glory for all eternity. Every pang of suffering is a golden milestone which marks your progress from the doing of the desires of the flesh, into the broad and boundless place of the will of God, whose length, breadth, height, and depth it will take all time to reveal, and all eternity to fulfill to its uttermost.

GUIDANCE

He leadeth me. PSALM 23:2

God guides us by His Word.

The Word of God is our supreme means of guidance. Wherever it speaks painly upon any problem the child of God need seek no further. For its authority is final. No Christian, for example, needs special guidance as to whether he is called to the consecration of his life to his Lord. The Word of God is absolutely clear in its call to all. Romans 12:1 is addressed to all believers and beseeches us as "brethren" to present our bodies a living sacrifice to God. So no believer needs special guidance as to whether he is called to live a holy life. The Word distinctly declares, "For this is the will of God, even your sanctification" (1 Th 4:3). No believer needs any special guidance against bitterness, censoriousness, and evil-speaking. The great command of God's Word is that we should love one another as Christ loved us. Wherever, therefore, the Word of God applies to our lives, its authority is supreme—and no guidance beyond it need be sought.

God may also guide us by circumstances.

God would not ordinarily lead a blind man to a work requiring great keenness of vision. Nor would He call a deaf man to a service demanding the sharpest of hearing. Neither would He lead an unlearned man to a translation work requiring a highly educated one. In such cases circumstances, unless they were changed, would seem to be conclusive guidance. Yet this is not true of all circumstances. For Satan may also enter this sphere of circumstances and so manipulate them as to woefully deceive even God's own children. The case of the Gibeonites is strikingly in point. God had warned Joshua to make no covenant with the Canaanites. But the Gibeonites were inhabitants of Canaan. So they devised a clever scheme to deceive Joshua and the princes of Israel into the belief that they were from a far-off land. To this end, among other things they brought moldy bread. This, they said, they had taken hot from their ovens when they started from their alleged distant home. The journey was so long that it had grown moldy by the way and they showed it to buttress their deception. Then follows the striking statement (Jos 9:14): "And the men (that is, the Israelites) took of their victuals and asked not counsel at the mouth of the Lord." That is, Joshua and his elders accepted the circumstance of the moldy bread as conclusive without testing it out in prayer and waiting upon God. The result was disastrous. They made a covenant with an enemy people contrary to the command of God. The teaching for the Christian here is luminously clear. Circumstances should ordinarily be tested in the place of waiting and the chamber of prayer in order that God may either confirm them as being of Himself or show us that they are being used by our great adversary to beguile us.

God also guides us by the Spirit.

Years ago a godly pastor named Blumhardt was greatly used of God in prayer for the healing of the sick. Ere he prayed for healing he was wont to wait upon God in prayer to ascertain His will as to healing the individual before him. He testified that when he first began to pray in this way it often took him hours to ascertain the will of God in the matter. But after a couple of years of coming to God in this way he stated that often he would scarcely turn to God in prayer ere the answer would come, almost instantly. He had learned by much experience to know the mind of God as to the healing of the sick one before him.

This illustrates what is probably the most important lesson for the Christian as to the guidance of the Spirit. It is that such guidance is learned only by a close, continuous, experimental walk with God, and in no other way. Such a walk is fraught with great blessing to the child of God. Any other is beset with peril. What that peril is the Word reveals when it says, "Try the spirits whether they are of God" (1 Jn 4:1). Plainly we are taught here, as elsewhere, that there are other spirits than the Spirit of God. These are spirits of evil. Their business is to deceive and lead astray. And only by such an experimental knowledge as the godly pastor named above had acquired can we ourselves be preserved from the danger of their insidious misleadings. How do you learn to recognize a human voice? Never from another's description of it. You must actually hear that voice again and again until you are able unerringly to recognize and distinguish it from all other voices. This was the way Blumhardt came to know his great Shepherd's voice. Nor is there any other way for us to know it, for

There is no royal road to guidance.

It is taught only in God's school. And there only can it be learned. We must be willing to sit on the primary benches, if necessary, to master all its lessons. For guidance is one of the severest tests of the Christian's walk with God. It touches his life at every point. Prayer, knowledge of the Word, personal temperament, tendency to haste, advice of friends, reliance upon our own wisdom, impatience with delays, submission to the will of God in all matters in question—all these and many more become factors in seeking guidance. They test to the limit our personal walk with God. No experience is more common in the believer's life than to come into the place of absolute perplexity as to which of two paths to take, which of two possible courses of action to follow. And while there are times when the crisis is met with comparative ease, there are others when our perplexity is extreme as to what we shall do at the parting of the ways. Then every lesson of prayer, experience, and knowledge of God's Word comes into play and helps to illumine our pathway and make clear our course of action.

God's great clarifier in guidance is waiting.

Sometimes you draw from the faucet a glass of water which is muddy and turbid. How do you clear it? You place the glass of muddy water on your table. Moment by moment the sediment deposits at the bottom of the glass. Gradually the water grows clearer. In a few moments it is so clear that you may distinguish objects through it. It was all brought about simply by waiting.

The law is the same in the realm of guidance. God's great precipitant is waiting. We face some situation needing His guidance. It is full of uncertainty. We seek to peer through it as through the glass of turbid water. But we cannot see. The one thing to do is to wait. As we do so the sediment slowly settles. The situation clears. Things take on new proportions, new adjustments. The trifling things assume their proper place of insignificance. The big things loom up into their proper importance. Waiting is the solution of it all. The time element is the supremely essential factor. The vast majority of our mistakes come from neglect of it. Haste is more often a trap of Satan than it is a necessity of guidance. "They which believe shall not make haste" is true here as in many other crises.

Guidance is sometimes extraordinary, sometimes ordinary.

Paul's guidance to the open door in Macedonia by the vision of the man who stood there beseeching him; Peter's vision of the sheet let down from heaven to show

76

the broadening of the gospel stream to the Gentiles; the disciples' guidance to the upper chamber for the passover by the man with the pitcher who led them to it; the wise men's guidance from the far-away East by the star which at length stood over the Christ child—all these are instances of extraordinary guidance. And all of us have had examples of such extraordinary guidance. Some great text flashes out of the Word to make our pathway luminous with its teaching; some striking circumstance rears itself in our path as a clear fingerboard of guidance; some strong, steadfast pressure of the Spirit stays with us until we see that it is clearly of God—all are cases of the extraordinary in guidance. Yet we need to remember that God also guides by the usual as well as the unusual. And it would spell disaster for us to insist upon the extraordinary when God may be leading us by the ordinary. The guidance of King Saul at the mouth of the prophet is a clear case of God combining the unusual with the usual. Saul was to meet two men at Rachel's tomb who would tell him of the finding of his father's straying herd. A little further on he would meet three men bearing provisions who would give to him from their supply. Still later would come a company of prophets, and their spirit of prophecy was to fall upon Saul who would himself prophesy. These were all cases of extraordinary guidance. But when these had come to pass—then, said Samuel, "Do as occasion serve thee" (1 Sa 10:7). That is, at this point the extraordinary guidance was to cease and the ordinary begin. Now he was to use his God-guided judgment concerning each circumstance as it arose, and take each step as occasion demanded. This brings us naturally to our next truth, namely, that

Guidance is usually a step at a time.

All of us need this lesson. We want our guidance as far in advance as possible instead of being content to walk with God a step at a time. Yet this is at once faith's

77

severest test and highest development. Most of our mistakes in guidance come from our wanting to see beyond the next turn in the road, or the next bend in the river. "I thank God for the tracklessness of the desert," said a devout child of God. It is a beautiful picture. The traveler who rises in the morning to traverse the great desert looks out upon a trackless waste. There is not a trace of a sign or a beaten path. There is but one thing for him to do. That is to follow his guide, step by step, through all the weary journey of the day over the untrodden waste. Such is the perfect walk of the child of God who has learned to trust Him. Such was Abraham's who went forth "not knowing whither he went" save that he was following the Guide who was leading him. Such is the lesson Christ brings to us when He says, "Are there not twelve hours in the day?" His life was so meted out by God that He lived every hour in His Father's plan and purpose taking no anxious thought for the morrow. And our Lord means this same lesson for us when He says, "As the Father hath sent me even so send I you" (Jn 20:21). Do we doubt this step-by-step guidance for the future? Then let us look back upon the years of the past. No child of God can do so without unspeakable gratitude and wonderment. For God has led him every faltering step of his way up to the very hour at which he reads these lines.

Guidance may be by stops as well as steps.

"The stops of a good man, as well as his steps, are ordered by the Lord," says George Muller. Naturally an opened door seems more like guidance to us than a closed one. Yet God may guide by the latter as definitely as by the former. His guidance of the children of Israel by the pillar of cloud and fire is a clear case in point (Numbers 9). When the cloud was lifted the Israelites took up their march. It was the guidance of God to move onward. But when the cloud tarried and abode upon the tabernacle

78

then the people rested in their tents. "Whether it were two days, or a month, or a year, that the cloud tarried the children of Israel abode in their tents, and journeyed not. ... At the commandment of the Lord they rested, and at the commandment of the Lord they journeyed (Num 9:21-22). Both the tarrying and the journeying were guidance from the Lord, the one as much as the other. We, when we are hindered or stayed from moving forward, are prone to think that we are having no guidance. In fact no guidance forward may be guidance of the most real sort. It is simply guidance to wait. Waiting, with the cloud, is true and blessed guidance. Going ahead without it is simply human willfulness.

Guidance is usually cumulative.

God does not confine our guidance to any one proof or leading, but confirms it by accumulative signs and indications. He not only led Saul to Ananias but prepared Ananias for Saul. He led Philip to the wilderness there to find someone whom he had prepared for Philip. He gives a message from the Word, and then leads us to those who need to hear it. He confirms the Word by the Spirit, and buttresses the inner guidance by external circumstances. He makes us fruitful in one service, and barren in another. He gives joy and blessing in the ministry He is drawing us *to*, and distaste and unrest in that He is leading us *from*. He forges one link after another in the chain of guidance until the whole is complete and convincing. Of this kind is the statement of Christ concerning prayer, that if two of His own be agreed touching anything it shall be given them. The truth here is better expressed in the thought "if two of you find yourselves agreed." If one of us is guided to a certain petition in prayer we might have some doubt as to our own leading in the matter. But when another believer, and then another is led the same way the proof becomes cumulative that our leading is coming from a common source,

79

namely, the Lord in the midst of us. The word "to be agreed" here is a musical expression meaning "to strike the same note." The truth is a beautiful one. For the unison of a great orchestra in striking the same note as it tunes up is proof conclusive that the common note came from its common leader. So when Spirit-led men and women find themselves "striking the same note" in their prayer petitions it is pretty sure proof that this note came from their own great Leader.

Beware of shortcuts in guidance.

We recall a summer day in Switzerland. A number of us were crossing a great glacier. The path was narrow and winding. Presently we came to a point where the guide, instead of continuing straight ahead, made a sharp, sudden detour to the right. Of course all of us followed his lead—that is, all but one man. He was evidently annoyed at the detour and resolved to take a shortcut. So he started straight ahead instead of following in the pathway. Immediately the guide rushed back, grasped him by the collar, and with no gentle hand dragged him back. Then, without a word, he pointed to a patch of snow upon which the man was about to tread. Instead of being a sure foothold for his steps, it was a mere crust of snow covering a great crevasse opening into the very bowels of the glacier. Had he trodden upon it he would have gone down to an unspeakable death into the heart of the great glacier. The shortcut would have ended in disaster.

A similar peril besets the believer's walk. Sometimes our Guide seems too slow for us. Haste of spirit, eagerness for results, counsel of well-meaning friends, seeming delay of God to lead us onward—these things and others of a kind tempt us to take shortcuts toward desired ends. But like the man on the glacier we make a mistake which may end in disaster. At times God does indeed seem to lead us by devious and roundabout paths. But it pays us far better to make detours *with* Him than to take short-cuts *without* Him.

Beware of guidance solely of the flesh.

Flesh and blood could not reveal the Christ to Simon Peter. Neither can it reveal the things of Christ to us. Nor does it matter whether it is our own flesh and blood or that of some other. For the other man's flesh and blood is compassed with the same infirmities and subject to the same errors as ours. Moreover the man who relies upon his friends for his guidance soon finds that the variety of advice they offer only increases the number of his perplexities. Then too it is a divine principle that God does not reveal to another man His plans for your life. Christ's rebuke of Peter for wanting to know His will for John is the clearest possible proof of this (Jn 21:22). You may help the little child to walk in its beginnings of the art. But if it is ever to learn to walk alone there comes a time when it must let go of your hand entirely and cease from all dependence upon you. The believer who would learn to walk with God must learn the same lesson. And as baby learns it at the cost of some tumbles, even so must the Christian learn it at the cost of some mistakes. It were better learned that way than not to be learned at all. The price of a few blunders is not too high for such a treasure as a walk alone with God in the place of His own guidance. Does God then have no place for your Christian friends in this matter of guidance? He surely does. Get all the help; all the light upon God's Word; all the experience of others you possibly can. You may get facts from others, but you must make your decisions yourself. For when we reach the place of decision we cannot evade the personal, patient waiting upon God alone through which we learn the most precious lessons of His guidance.

Guidance is sure for those who wait and pray.

Sometimes our perplexity is so great that it seems no guidance will ever come. For such times the psalmist has a precious message in his word about the night watchers. "My soul waiteth for the Lord more than they that watch for the morning" (Ps 130:6). How do men who wait in the night hours for the dawn watch for the morning? The answer is fourfold.

1. They watch in *darkness*.
2. They watch for that which *comes slowly*.
3. They watch for that which is *sure to come*.
4. They watch for that which when it does come *brings the light of day*.

So is it with us who wait for guidance. Often our perplexity is so extreme that we seem to be waiting in total darkness. Often too as we wait, even as those who wait for the day, the first faint streaks of dawn seem to come, *oh so slowly!* Then too as there never yet has been a night which was not sure to end in the dawn, so our night of uncertainty is sure to end in the dawning light of God's guidance. Lastly, as the slow coming dawn, when it does arrive, brings light and blessing without measure, so when our God-given guidance at last breaks upon us it will so rejoice our waiting souls and so illumine our beclouded path we shall almost forget the long days when we waited in darkness; waited for that which was so slow in coming; yet waited for that which was as sure to come as the tender radiance of the dawn was sure to those who watched and waited for the morning.

THE GOD-PLANNED LIFE

Created in Christ Jesus unto good works, which God hath before ordained that we should walk in them.

EPHESIANS 2:10

"Created in Christ Jesus": that means every child of God is a new creation in Christ Jesus. "Unto good works." And that means every such child of God is created anew in Christ Jesus for a life of service. "Which God hath before ordained." That means God has laid the plan for this life of service in Christ Jesus, ages before we came into existence. "That we should walk in them." "Walk" is a practical word. And that means God's purpose of service for the lives of his children is not a mere fancy, but a practical reality, to be known and lived out in our present work-a-day life. Therefore all through this great text runs the one supreme thought that

God has a plan for every life in Christ Jesus.

What a wondrous truth is this! And yet how reasonable a one. Shall the architect draw the plans for his stately palace? Shall the artist sketch the outlines of his masterpiece? Shall the shipbuilder lay down the lines for his colossal ship? And yet shall God have no plan for the immortal soul which He brings into being and puts "in Christ Jesus"? Surely he has. Yea, for every cloud that floats across the summer sky; for every blade of grass that points its tiny spear heavenward; for every dewdrop that gleams in the morning sun; for every beam of light that shoots across the limitless space from sun to earth, God has a purpose and a plan. How much more then,

83

for you who are His own, in Christ Jesus, does God have a perfect before-prepared life plan. And not only so, but

God has a plan for your life which no other man can fulfil.

"In all the ages of the ages there never has been, and never will be a man, or woman just like me. I am unique. I have no double." That is true. No two leaves, no two jewels, no two stars, no two lives—alike. Every life is a fresh thought from God to the world. There is no man in all the world who can do your work as well as you. And if you do not find and enter into God's purpose for your life, there will be something missing from the glory that would otherwise have been there. Every jewel gleams with its own radiance. Every flower distils its own fragrance. Every Christian has his own particular bit of Christ's radiance and Christ's fragrance which God would pass through him to others. Has God given you a particular personality? He has also created a particular circle of individuals who can be reached and touched by that personality as by none other in the wide world. And then He shapes and orders your life so as to bring you into contact with that very circle. Just a hair's breadth of shift in the focus of the telescope, and some man sees a vision of beauty which before had been all confused and befogged. So, too, just that grain of individual and personal variation in your life from every other man's and someone sees Jesus Christ with a clearness and beauty he would discern nowhere else. What a privilege to have one's own Christ-indwelt personality, however humble! What a joy to know that God will use it, as He uses no other for certain individuals susceptible to it as to no other! In you there is just a bit of change in the angle of the jewel—and lo, some man sees the light! In you there is just a trifle of variation in the mingling of the spices—and, behold, someone becomes conscious of the fragrance of Christ.

A man may fail to enter God's plan for his life.

Among the curiosities of a little fishing village on the great lakes where we were summering was a pair of captive eagles. They had been captured when but two weeks old, and confined in a large roomlike cage. Year after year the eaglets grew, until they were magnificent specimens of their kind, stretching six feet from tip to tip of wings. One summer when we came back for our usual vacation the eagles were missing. Inquiring of the owner as to their disappearance this story came to us. The owner had left the village for a prolonged fishing trip out in the lake. While he was absent some mischievous boys opened the door of the cage, and gave the great birds their liberty. At once they endeavored to escape. But kept in captivity from their earliest eaglet days, they had never learned to fly. They seemed to realize that God had meant them to be more than mere earthlings. After all these weary years the instinct for the sky and the heavens still smoldered in their hearts. And most desperately did they strive to exercise it. They floundered about upon the village green. They struggled, and fell, and beat their wings in piteous efforts to rise into the airy freedom of their God-appointed destiny. But all in vain. One of them, essaying to fly across a small stream, fell helpless into the water and had to be rescued from drowning. The other, after a succession of desperate and humiliating failures managed to attain to the lowermost limb of a nearby tree. Thence he was shot to death by the hand of a cruel boy. His mate soon shared the same hapless fate. And the simple tragedy of their hampered lives came to an end.

Often since has come to us the tragic life lesson of the imprisoned eagles. God had designed for these kingly birds a noble inheritance of freedom. It was theirs to pierce in royal flights the very eye of the midday sun. It was theirs to nest in lofty crags where never foot of man had trod. It was theirs to breast with unwearying pinion the storms and tempests of mid-heaven. A princely heritage indeed was theirs. But the cruelty of man had hopelessly shut them out from it. And instead of the limitless liberty planned for them had come captivity, helplessness, humiliation, and death. Even these birds of the air missed God's great plan for their lives. Much more may the sons of men.

Is not this the very thing of which Paul speaks when he says: "Work out your own salvation with fear and trembling, for it is God which worketh in you both to will and to do of his good pleasure" (Phil 2:12-13). What are these inner voices which, if we heed not, cease? What are these visions which, if we follow not, fade? What are these yearnings to be all for Christ which, if we embody not in action, die? What are they but the living God working in us to will and to do the life-work which he has planned for us from all eternity? And it is this which you are called upon to "work out." Work it out in love. Work it out in daily, faithful ministry. Work it out as God works in you. But more than that. You may miss it. You may fall short of God's perfect plan for your life. Therefore work it out with—fear and trembling! Searching words are these. Words of warning, words of tender admonition. That blessed life of witnessing, serving, and fruit-bearing which God has planned for you in Christ Jesus from all eternity—work it out *with trembling*. Trembling—lest the god of this world blind you to the vision of service which God is ever holding before you. Trembling—lest the low standard of life in fellow Christians about you lead you to drop yours to a like grovelling level. Trembling—lest some little circle in the dark ends of the earth should fail of the giving, the praying, or the going which God has long since planned for you. Trembling—lest the voices of worldly pleasure and ambition dull and deafen your ears to the one voice which is ever whispering, "follow thou Me; follow thou *Me*."

*One way of missing God's calling may be by "choosing"
our own calling.*

Every day men talk of "choosing" a calling. But is not
the phrase a sheer misnomer? For how can a man "choose"
a "calling"? If a man is called *he* does not choose. It is the
one who calls who does the choosing. "Ye have not chosen
Me but *I* have chosen *you* and ordained you that ye
should go and bear fruit," says our Lord. Men act as
though God threw down before them an assortment of
plans from which they might choose what pleases them,
even as a shopkeeper tosses out a dozen skeins of silk
to a lady buyer from which she might select that which
strikes her fancy. But it is not true. It is God's to choose.
It is ours simply to ascertain and obey. For next in
its eternal moment to the salvation of the soul is the guidance of the life of a child of God. And God claims both
as His supreme prerogative. The man who trusts God
with one, but wrests from Him the other, is making a
fatal mistake. Would we were taught this ere our unskilled
hand had time to mar the plan! In default of such teaching
let us confess with humbled hearts the mistakes we have
made here, in the frailty of our mere human judgment.

Young friend, are you standing in that trying place
where men are pressing you to "choose" a calling? Are
you about to cast the die of a *self-chosen* life work? Do
not cast it. Do not *try* to choose. Does not the text say
we are created *in* Christ unto good works? If the plan is
in Christ how will you find it unless you go *to* Christ?
Therefore go to God simply, trustfully, prayerfully and ask
Him to show you what He has chosen for you from all
eternity. And as you walk in the daily light which He
sheds upon your path He will surely lead you into His
appointed life-plan.. So shall you be saved the sorrow,
disappointment, and failure which follow in the wake of
him who "chooses" his own path, and, all too late, comes
to himself to find out that it pays to trust God in this
great concern of his life, even as in all others.

Every child of God may find and enter into God's plan for his life.

You remember the story of the engineer of the Brooklyn bridge. During its building he was injured. For many long months he was shut up in his room. His gifted wife shared his toils, and carried his plans to the workmen. At last the great bridge was completed. Then the invalid architect asked to see it. They put him upon a cot and carried him to the bridge. They placed him where he could see the magnificent structure in all its beauty. There he lay, in his helplessness, intently scanning the work of his genius. He marked the great cables, the massive piers, the mighty anchorages which fettered it to the earth. His critical eye ran over every beam, every girder, every chord, every rod. He noted every detail carried out precisely as he had dreamed it in his dreams, and wrought it out in his plans and specifications. And then as the joy of achievement filled his soul, as he saw and realized that it was finished exactly as he had designed it, in an ecstasy of delight he cried out, "it's just like the plan; *it's just like the plan.*"

Some day we shall stand in the glory and looking up into His face, cry out, "O God, I thank Thee that Thou didst turn me aside from my willful and perverse way to Thy loving and perfect one. I thank Thee that Thou didst ever lead me to yield my humble life to Thee. I thank Thee that as I day by day walked the simple pathway of service, Thou didst let me gather up one by one the golden threads of Thy great purpose for my life. I thank Thee, as, like a tiny trail creeping its way up some great mountainside, that pathway of life has gone on in darkness and light, storm and shadow, weakness and tears, failures and falterings, Thou hast at last brought me to its destined end. And now that I see my finished life, no longer 'through a glass darkly' but in the face to face splendor of Thine own glory, I thank Thee, O God, I thank Thee that it's just like the plan; *it's just like the plan.*"

Then, too, while we do need to walk carefully and

earnestly that we miss not God's great will for us, yet let us not be anxious lest, because we are so human, so frail, so fallible, we may make some mistakes in the details and specifications of that plan. For we will do well to remember this. God has a beautiful way of overruling mistakes when the heart is right with Him. That is the supreme essential. The one attitude of ours which can mar His purpose of love for our lives is the refusal to yield that life and will to His own great will of love for it. But when that life is honestly yielded, then the mistakes in the pathway which spring from our own human infirmities and fallibleness will be sweetly and blessedly corrected by God, as we move along that path. It is like guiding a ship. Our trembling hand upon the wheel may cause trifling wanderings from her course. But they seem greater to us than they are in reality. And if we but hold our craft steadily to the polestar of God's will, as best we know it, she will reach her destined port with certainty, notwithstanding the swervings that have befallen her in the progress of her voyage.

But now we come face to face with a question of supreme importance: "How shall I ascertain God's plan for my life? How shall I be safeguarded from error? How shall I discern the guidance of God from the misguidance of my own fleshly desires and ambitions? How shall I find the path in which He is calling me to walk?"

Believe God has a life-plan for you.

The trouble with most of us is that we do not believe God has such a life-plan for us. We take our own way, we lay our own plans, we choose our own profession, we decide upon our own business without taking God into account at all. "According to our faith is it unto us." And if we have no faith in God's word in this regard, what else can we expect but to miss God's way for our lives, and only come back to it after long and costly wanderings from His blessed, chosen pathway for us?

Ephesians 2:10 is as surely inspired as Ephesians 2:8. The promise of a life-plan is as explicit in the one as the promise of salvation is in the other. Brood over this Ephesian verse. Is it plain? Is it God's word? Does it not say clearly that God has a life-plan for you in Christ Jesus? Then settle down upon it. Believe it with your whole soul. Do not be shaken from it.

Pray for wisdom concerning God's plan.

Dr. Henry Foster, founder of the Clifton Springs sanatorium, was a man of marvelous power with God—a man, too, of great insight into the mind and ways of God in the matter of guidance in the affairs of life. What was the secret of that wondrous power and wisdom? Visitors were wont to ask this question of one of the older physicians on the staff of that great institution. And this was his response. He took the visitor by the arm. He led him upstairs to the door of Dr. Foster's office. He led him into this little chamber, across to the corner of the room. There, kneeling, he lifted up the border of a rug and showed to the visitor two ragged holes in the carpet, worn by the knees of God's saint in his life of prayer. "That, sir, was the secret of Henry Foster's power and wisdom in the things of God and men."

Friend, when your bedroom carpet begins to wear out after that fashion, the man who lives in that room need not have any fear about missing God's life-plan. For that is the open secret of wisdom and guidance in the life of every man who knows anything about walking with God. "Does any man lack wisdom? Let him *ask* of God." Are you one of the men who lack wisdom concerning God's plan for their lives? Then ask of God. Pray! Pray trustfully, pray steadily, pray expectantly, and God will certainly guide you into that blessed place where you will be as sure you are in His chosen pathway as you are of your salvation.

Will to do God's Will.

Will what? Will to do *God's* will for your life, instead of your own. Do not launch out upon the sea of life headed for a port of your own choosing, guided by a chart of your own drafting, driven by the power of your own selfish pleasures or ambitions. Come to God. Yield your life to Him by one act of trustful, irrevocable surrender. And then begin to choose and to do His will for your life instead of your own. So shall you come steadily to know and see God's will for that life. Our Lord Jesus said this clearly: "If any man will to do his will he shall know" (Jn 7:17). Without a shadow of doubt, we will begin to know God's will as soon as we begin to choose His will for our lives instead of our own.

Thus the spiritual fieldglasses through which we come to see God's will for our lives are double-barreled. Side by side are two lenses. The one—"I trust." The other—"I will." When a man can hold both of these to his eyes he will see God's will with unclouded clearness. But suppose a man says to God, "I doubt." Then a veil falls over that lens of faith. And suppose he says, "I will not." Then the veil falls over the other, the lens of the will, of choice. Straightway that man's spiritual vision is in eclipse. He walks in a darkness of his own making, springing from his own unfaith and self-will, yet the source and cause of which he, in his blindness, wholly fails to perceive.

Friend, are you walking in such darkness? Is there such a veil between you and the will of God for your life? Listen. Begin to *believe* in God's plan for your life. That veil will become translucent. Begin to *will* to do God's will. That veil will become transparent. Begin, day by day, actually to *do* God's will. That veil will vanish! And when it is gone, and you are walking in the full light of God's will for your life you will see that it was self-will alone which shut out the clear vision of God's will. For no man can see the will of God save through

91

these two crystal lenses—the trustful heart and the yielded will.

Does someone say at this point: "But suppose I have given my life to God to enter into His will for it. What change shall I make in it? Shall I seek a new environment, a new sphere? What shall I do? We answer

Stay where you are, and do the next thing.

Talk God's plan, and consecration to it, to Christian men and straightway many of them think you mean them to give up their business and head at once for the pulpit or the foreign missionary field. To come into God's life-plan is to go into some other *place,* as they view it. But there never was a greater mistake. Consecration is not necessarily dislocation. Not by any means. God's plan for a man's life does not of necessity lift him out from his present realm of life and surroundings. It is not a new sphere God is seeking. It is a new man in the present sphere! It is not transference. It is transformation. The trouble is not usually with the place. It is with the man in the place. And when a man consecrates his life to God to find and enter into God's perfect plan for that life, God will *usually* keep him right where he is, but living for God and His kingdom instead of living for self. So, until God shows you differently, stay where you are, and live for Him.

If God wants you elsewhere, He will lead you there; be sure to follow.

We have seen that consecration is not necessarily dislocation. Yet it *may* be. God usually keeps a man where he is when he yields his life to him. Yet *not always*. God may lift you from the sphere in which you are moving. God may completely change your environment, as well as change you. God may take you out of your business or profession, and send you to the uttermost parts of the earth as a chosen messenger of His. But how will this come about, you ask. *As you do the next thing.* The golden chain of God's great purpose for your life and mine is woven of the single links which we lay hold of, one at a time, along the pathway of daily opportunity. By and by, when we have gathered enough links, the chain begins to appear. The man who faithfully picks up the links need never fear about missing the chain. Therefore do the next thing. As you do it this thread of daily service becomes in God's hands like the clue to a maze. By it God leads you on in your pathway until you are out from all the labyrinth of darkness and uncertainty, into the clear shining of His will for your life. Therefore do it patiently, faithfully, lovingly. Teach the class, visit the sick, comfort the sorrowing, preach the Word, use the tract and leaflet, witness for Him just where you are. And as you thus serve, if God wants you elsewhere, He will surely lead you there. Only *be sure to follow.* And thus following some of us will land in China, India, Africa. And some of us will abide just where we are. But all of us will be where He wants us. And that is *in the plan.*

"As," says someone, "this is all very well for the young and the strong who have all of life before them. But it is too late for me. My life has been full of blunders and failures. It is only after years of wandering that I have come to Christ. There is nothing left for me but the memory of mistakes and the fragments of a vanished and broken life." Listen, friend, to the truth that

God is the only one who can take a seemingly shattered life and make a beautiful life from the fragments.

Have you ever heard this story? In a certain old town was a great cathedral. And in that cathedral was a wondrous stained glass window. Its fame had gone abroad over the land. From miles around people pilgrimaged to gaze upon the splendor of this masterpiece of art. One day there came a great storm. The violence of the tempest forced in the window and it crashed to the marble floor, shattered into a hundred pieces. Great was the grief of the people at the catastrophe which had suddenly bereft the town of its proudest work of art. They gathered up the fragments, hudddled them in a box, and carried them to the cellar of the church. One day there came along a stranger who asked permission to see the beautiful window. They told him of its fate. He asked what they had done with the fragments. And they took him to the vault and showed him the broken glass. "Would you mind giving these to me?" said the stranger. "Take them along," was the reply, "they are no longer of any use to us." And the visitor carefully lifted the box and carried it away in his arms. Weeks passed by; then one day there came an invitation to the custodians of the cathedral. It was from a famous artist, noted for his skill in glassworking. It summoned them to his study to inspect a stained glass window, the work of his genius. Ushering them into his studio he stood them before a great veil of canvass. At the touch of his hand upon a cord the canvass dropped. And there before their astonished gaze shone a stained glass window surpassing in beauty all their eyes had ever beheld. As they gazed upon its rich tints, wondrous pattern, and cunning workmanship, the artist turned and said, "This window I have wrought from the fragments of your shattered one, and it is now ready to be replaced." Once more a great window shed its beauteous light into the dim aisles of the old cathedral. But the splendor of the new far surpassed the glory of the old, and the fame of its strange fashioning filled the land.

Reader, do you say that your plans have been crushed? Thank God and take heart. Have you not long since learned that the best place for many of your plans is the trash pile? And that often you must fling them there before your blinded eyes can see God's own better plan for your life? And how is it with your life? Has sin blighted it? Have the mistakes of early years seemingly wrecked it? Have joy and sweetness vanished from it? Does there seem nought left for you but to walk its weary treadmill until its days of darkness and drudgery shall end? Then know this. Jesus Christ is a matchless life-mender. *Try Him.* He will take that seemingly shattered life and fashion a far more beautiful one from its fragments than you yourself could ever have wrought from the whole. In Him your weary soul shall find its longed-for rest. And the fragments that remain of God's heritage of life to you shall mean, in gladsome days to come, more than all the vanished years that croon their sad lament in your innermost soul.

> Why do I drift on a storm-tossed sea,
> With neither compass, nor star, nor chart,
> When, as I drift, God's own plan for me,
> Waits at the door of my slow-trusting heart?
>
> Down from the heavens it drops like a scroll,
> Each day a bit will the Master unroll,
> Each day a mite of the veil will He lift,
> Why do I falter? Why wonder, and drift?
>
> Drifting, while God's at the helm to steer;
> Groping, when God lays the course, so clear;
> Swerving, though straight into port I might sail;
> Wrecking, when heaven lies just within hail.
>
> Help me, O God, in the plan to believe:
> Help me my fragment each day to receive,
> Oh that my will may with Thine have no strife!
> God-yielded wills find the God-planned life.

CHASTENING

Whom the Lord loveth he chasteneth.   HEBREWS 12:6

How deep is the mystery of God's chastening of His children! And how the soul shrinks at the very mention of the word! Yet, in this Hebrews passage is set forth some of the most precious teaching of God's Word as to His loving dealing with the lives of His own. Let us give heed to it. For it touches the deeps of Christian experience in that it brings us face to face with God's wondrous grace in overruling the mystery of suffering to the enrichment and unspeakable blessing of the lives of His children.

Chastening is God's "child-training."

That is what the word means. It is built upon the Greek word *child*. It is the rootword for *child* with the verb termination added to it. It means "to deal with as a child," to "child-train." Nine times in the passage occurs the word *son, child,* and *father.* God is speaking to His own. We are His own dear children. He has brought us into His great family. And now having saved us, He is going to train us. Up there is the homeland and the glory; down here is the suffering. He is even overruling the suffering to child-train us for the glory. And thus what sweetness and preciousness flow forth from this much misunderstood fragment of His Word as we invest it with this its literal significance. Let us read it into the whole passage and mark the blessing in it.

"My son, despise not thou the chastening of the Lord, nor faint when thou art rebuked of him: for whom the Lord loveth he chasteneth, and scourgeth every son whom he receiveth. If ye endure chastening, God dealeth with

you as with sons; for what son is he whom the father chasteneth not? But if ye be without chastisement, whereof all are partakers, then are ye bastards, and not sons. Furthermore we have had fathers of our flesh which corrected us, and we gave them reverence: shall we not much rather be in subjection to the Father of spirits, and live? For they verily for a few days chastened us after their own pleasure; but he for our profit, that we might be partakers of his holiness. Now no chastening for the present seemeth to be joyous, but grievous: nevertheless afterward it yieldeth the peaceable fruit of righteousness unto them which are exercised thereby" (Heb 12:5-11).

Chastening is for purification.

Does God have a grudge against us? Is God trying, as it were, to "get even" with us? Is God's "child-training" a kind of parental revenge for childish wrongdoing? Often we think so. But it is far from the truth. "For they (our earthly parents) verily for a few days child-trained us after their own pleasure; but he FOR OUR PROFIT, that we might be PARTAKERS OF HIS HOLINESS" (v. 10). God's one supreme purpose in child-training us is purification. He is seeking to purge from us all that mars the likeness of Jesus Christ within us. It is His own holiness that He is seeking to perfect within us.

A visitor was watching a silversmith heating the silver in his crucible. Hotter and hotter grew the fires. All the while the smith was closely scanning the crucible. Presently the visitor said, "Why do you watch the silver so closely? What are you looking for?" "I am looking for my face," was the answer. "When I see my own image in the silver, then I stop. The work is done." Why did the silversmith light the fires under the silver? To purify and perfect it. Is God's child-training an executioner visiting upon us the wrath of God? Nay, it is rather a cleansing angel pouring forth upon us the love of God. The furnace, the suffering, the agony of child-training, what do they mean? *God is looking for a face!* It is the face of His Son. For He has foreordained us to be conformed to the image of His Son (Ro 8:29). And He is purging from us in child-training all that dims that image. Therefore, child of God, do not associate chastening only with the word *chastise.* Couple it also with that beautiful word *chastity,* the jewel of perfect, spotless purity of heart and life. Thus *chasten* is to *chaste-en.* It is to make chaste, to make pure, spiritually. To purge, to cleanse, to purify—that is God's great purpose in all His "child-training."

Like all true parents, therefore, God has a model, a pattern to which He is fashioning the lives of His children. That pattern is Jesus Christ. And God's great purpose is that Christ should be formed in us. Thus the will of the Father is perfect. But the will of the child must be plastic. For how can the will of the Father be carried out unless the will of the child be yielded? Otherwise may not the child baffle at every step the highest purpose of the Father for the life of the child? You can do anything with an obedient child. You can do nothing with a disobedient one. Wherefore *the first great lesson God is seeking to teach in chastening is obedience.*

Chastening results in obedience.

"Though he were a Son yet learned he obedience by the things which he suffered" (Heb 5:8) is the wondrous word spoken of the Lord Himself. And have you not noted how true this is in the lives of all God's children? The chamber of suffering—is it not the birthplace of obedience? Is not the crowning grace of utter submission to His will wrought out in the place of affliction as nowhere else? Go sometimes into such a chamber of suffering. There lies one of God's "shut-ins." For years she has been in the fiery furnace of affliction. By and by you express the hope that this affliction may pass away. A smile flits over the wan face. Quickly from the trembling

98

lips drops this sentence: "If it be God's will." Not her own will, but God's! That is the first thought. The words, the spirit, the life of the sufferer all image forth one great truth—absolute submission to the will of God. Somehow —we know not how—but, *somehow,* this spirit of obedience, of perfect submission to the will of God is wrought out in the furnace and the crucible as in no other experience of life. How many of us strong-willed men and women have found that to be true!

We recall a striking story from the lips of a friend. A lady was summering in Switzerland. One day she started out for a stroll. Presently, as she climbed the mountainside, she came to a shepherd's fold. She walked to the door and looked in. There sat the shepherd. Around him lay his flock. Near at hand, on a pile of straw, lay a single sheep. It seemed to be suffering. Scanning it closely, the lady saw that its leg was broken. At once her sympathy went out to the suffering sheep. She looked up inquiringly to the shepherd. "How did it happen?" she said. To her amazement, the shepherd answered, "Madam, I broke that sheep's leg." A look of pain swept over the visitor's face. Seeing it, the shepherd went on, "Madam, of all the sheep in my flock, this one was the most wayward. It never would obey my voice. It never would follow in the pathway in which I was leading the flock. It wandered to the verge of many a perilous cliff and dizzy abyss. And not only was it disobedient itself, but it was ever leading the other sheep of my flock astray. I had before had experience with sheep of this kind. So I broke its leg. The first day I went to it with food, it tried to bite me. I let it lie alone for a couple of days. Then, I went back to it. And now, it not only took the food, but licked my hand, and showed every sign of submission and even affection. And now let me tell you something. When this sheep is well, as it soon will be, it will be the model sheep of my flock. No sheep will hear my voice so quickly. None will follow so closely at my side. Instead of leading its mates astray, it will now be an example and a guide for the wayward ones, leading them, with itself, in the path of obedience to my call. In short, a complete transformation will have come into the life of this wayward sheep. It has learned obedience through its suffering."

Friend, from the suffering of baffled plans which have brought you the keenest disappointment of life; from the suffering of personal bereavements which have torn from your presence loved ones unspeakably precious to your soul; from the suffering of temporal losses and broken fortunes; from the suffering which has stalked into your life through the willfulness and sin of others; from the suffering which seemed at times to bring you to the brink of a broken faith and a broken heart; yea, suffering one, out of your very agony of heart and soul, somehow, oh, somehow, the eternal God of love and mercy is seeking to bring into your life the supremest blessing that can enrich and glorify that life—the blessing of a human will yielded to the will of God.

And to be yielded to the will of God—what a place is that for you! It means more than silver and gold; more than gratified desires and ambition; more than all the sweet blandishments of friendship; more than all the praises of men; more than all the prizes of fame; yea, more than the attainment of all your highest earthly aims and strivings is this richest and deepest of all blessings, to be hidden, sunken, swallowed up in the will of God for all time and amid all circumstances. And it is that God is seeking to teach you through chastening. It is into this hiding place of peace and power from which the world can never dislodge you, that God is striving to bring you by the way of tribulation, disappointment and pain. All that brings you there is worth its costliest price of blood and suffering. Rather than the life out of His will nothing can be too dear-bought that brings us into that will. Rather than miss it, we can spare nothing from our lives that will compass it.

And now, as God brings us into this place of obedience,

He is able to work out in us the next rich outcome of His child-training.

Chastening results in fruitage.

"*Afterward it yieldeth . . . fruit*" (v. 11). The summer showers are falling. The poet stands by the window watching them. They are beating and buffeting the earth with their fierce downpour. But the poet sees in his imaginings more than the showers which are falling before his eyes. He sees myriads of lovely flowers which shall soon be breaking forth from the watered earth, filling it with matchless beauty and fragrance. And so he sings:

It isn't raining rain for me, it's raining daffodils;
In every dimpling drop I see wild flowers upon the hills.
A cloud of gray engulfs the day, and overwhelms the town;
It isn't raining rain for me: it's raining roses down.

Perchance one of God's chastened children is even now saying, "O God, it is raining hard for me tonight. Testings are raining upon me which seem beyond my power to endure. Disappointments are raining fast, to the utter defeat of all my chosen plans. Bereavements are raining into my life which are making my shrinking heart quiver in its intensity of suffering. The rain of affliction is surely beating down upon my soul these days." Withal, friend, you are mistaken. It isn't raining rain for you. It's raining blessing. For, if you will but believe your Father's word, under that beating rain are springing up spiritual flowers of such fragrance and beauty, as never before grew in that stormless, unchastened life of yours. You indeed see the rain. But do you see, also, the flowers? You are pained by the testings. But God sees the sweet flower of faith which is upspringing in your life under those very trials. You shrink from the suffering. But God sees the tender compassion for other sufferers which is finding birth in your soul. You see the disappointments, but God sees the sweet submission to His divine and

101

perfect will which is growing out of the very same. Your heart winces under the sore bereavement. But God sees the deepening and enriching which that sorrow has brought to you. It isn't raining afflictions for you. It is raining tenderness, love, compassion, patience, and a thousand other flowers and fruits of the blessed Spirit which are bringing into your life such a spiritual enrichment as all the fullness of worldly prosperity and ease was never able to beget in your innermost soul.

And are you saying, "But, what a fruitless branch I must be that God must needs so to purge me"? Nay, not so. Have you not noticed what kind of branches it is that God purges? Hear His word: "Every branch that *beareth fruit,* he purgeth it" (Jn 15:2). It is not the fruitless but the fruitful branch which is purged. And why? "That it may bring forth more fruit." Purging is, therefore, not the proof of worthlessness, but the proof of fruit. For it is only the fruit bearers that are purged. The others are taken away. Wherefore His purging is both the proof that there is fruit, and the pledge that there shall be more.

God does not expect us to enjoy chastening, but to endure it for the sake of its afterward.

Sometimes we reproach ourselves because we are not *enjoying* affliction. We ought to be like Paul, who, we say, "rejoiced in tribulation." But do we think by this that Paul really *enjoyed* tribulation? Surely not. When they flogged his naked back with the iron points of the leather-thonged scourge, do you think he enjoyed it? The stones they hurled at him were businesslike, merciless, jagged, and went home to their target with blows that crushed him into bloody insensibility. Think you he enjoyed that? The "perils by false brethren too"—do you know what that is? To have a friend play you false—one whom you had taken to your heart of hearts, one whom you leaned upon, and to whom you poured out your soul, what is that but the stiletto-stab that makes the blood spurt from every vein in your innermost being? Did you enjoy that? Surely

102

not. Well, neither did Paul. Neither does any man with flesh, and blood, and nerves, and heart. But what did this old hero of Jesus Christ's kingdom say about the affliction? Listen, "We glory in tribulations also: knowing that tribulations worketh patience," etc. (Rom. 5:3). He rejoiced not in tribulation itself, but amid tribulation for the things that came forth from it. Likewise, God, our Father, does not expect us to enjoy child-training. He is not displeased if we find it hard to bear, and shrink under it. Nay, He distinctly says, "it is grievous," and he only asks us to endure it, not for itself, but for the glorious "afterward" which is to come forth from it.

There are three warnings we need amid child-training: "despise not . . . nor faint" (Heb 12:5) and question not (Heb 12:9-10).

Despise not chastening.

Do not "esteem lightly" God's child-training. Do not look down upon it. Above all, do not let your heart grow hard and bitter against God because of it. Very needful is this warning to all of us. How many have lost fellowship with God, and have drifted into the dark places of doubt, rebelliousness, and despair because they have suffered their hearts to be embittered against God for His seemingly strange dealings with them! Ah! Friend, shun *that* above everything else. Harden not your heart. Do not rise up in mutiny of spirit against God. When you let *that* serpent coil in your heart, it will sting your innermost soul to the death of peace, and rest, and joy in your Lord. Guard yourself against that.

In the same verse, comes the warning to faint not.

Faint not when you are chastened.

How great is the temptation at this point! How the soul sinks, the heart grows sick, and the faith staggers under the keen trials and testings which come into our lives in times of special bereavement and suffering. "I cannot bear up any longer; I am fainting under this providence. What shall I do?" God tells me not to faint. "But what can one do when he is fainting?" What do you do when you are about to faint physically? You cannot do anything. You cease from your own doing. In your faintness, you fall upon the shoulder of some strong loved one. You lean hard. You rest. You lie still and trust, until your fainting soul comes back to its own. It is so when we are tempted to faint under affliction. God's message to us is not, "Be strong and of good courage," for He knows our strength and courage have fled away. But it is that sweet word, "Be still, and know that I am God." Hudson Taylor was so feeble in the closing months of his life, that he wrote a dear friend, "I am so weak I cannot work; I cannot read my Bible; I cannot even pray. I can only lie still in God's arms like a little child, and trust." This wondrous man of God with all his spiritual power came to a place of physical suffering and weakness where he could only lie still and trust. And that is all God asks of you, His dear child, when you grow faint in the fierce fires of affliction. Do not try to *be strong*. Just *be still,* and *know that He is God* and will sustain you, and bring you through.

There is a third warning we need in chastening.

Question not God's chastening.

There are some questions the believer may ask of his God. We may say "what" to God. For that is the question of service. "Lord, what wilt thou have me to do?" It is fair for us to ask that, for we have a right to know the particular ministry He has for us from day to day, even as had Paul. Again, we may say "where" to God. For that is the question of guidance. It is but right that we should know the place of our service; where He would have us walk, as we move on in our daily journey with our Lord. Then, too, we may say "when" to Him. For that is the question of time. And it is well to know His time for all things, that we neither run before Him in our zeal nor lag behind Him in our slothfulness. But there is one question no child of His should ever put to God concerning God's dealings with him in chastening. No man should ever say "why" to God. For "why" is the question of doubt. It is the assassin of faith. It leads us to the brink of a dizzy cliff—the precipice of rebellion against God. No Christian can afford to say it. Our Lord never uttered it save once, "My God, my God, *why* hast Thou forsaken me?" That awful *why*. It had all His life been a stranger to His lips. And why had it fallen now? Because of sin—not His, for He had none. But yours and mine, and the world's, which plunged Him, our sin-bearer, into the black despair of the only hour of separation from God He had ever known in all His eternal existence. And you and I are coming close to sin, with its darkness and broken fellowship, and its rebellion against God when we begin to question Him mistrustingly. You do not like your little one to say *why* to you, do you? Its mistrust wounds your father-soul. Neither would God have you say it to Him, for it brings like grief to His father-heart.

There are some other things for us to remember, too, in chastening.

Remember the love of God.

In an African mine was found the most magnificent diamond in the world's history. It was presented to the king of England to blaze in his crown of state. The king sent it to Amsterdam to be cut. It was put in the hands of an expert lapidary. And what do you suppose he did with it? He took this gem of priceless value. He cut a notch in it. Then he struck it a hard blow with his instrument and lo, the superb jewel lay in his hand, cleft in twain. What recklessness! What wastefulness! What criminal carelessness! Not so. For days and weeks that blow had been studied and planned. Drawings and models had been made of the gem. Its quality, its defects, its lines of cleavage had all been studied with minutest care. The man to whom it was committed was one of the most skillful lapidaries in the world. Do you say that blow was a mistake? Nay. It was the climax of the lapidary's skill. When he struck that blow, he did the one thing which would bring that gem to its most perfect shapeliness, radiance, and jewelled splendor. That blow which seemed to ruin the superb precious stone was in fact its perfect redemption. For, from these two halves were wrought the two magnificent gems which the skilled eye of the lapidary saw hidden in the rough, uncut stone as it came from the mines.

So, sometimes, God lets a stinging blow fall upon your life. The blood spurts. The nerves wince. The soul cries out in an agony of wondering protest. The blow seems to you an appalling mistake. But it is not, for you are the most priceless jewel in the world to God. And He is the most skilled lapidary in the universe. Some day you are to blaze in the diadem of the King. As you lie in His hand now He knows just how to deal with you. Not a blow will be permitted to fall upon your shrinking soul but that the love of God permits it, and works out from it depths of blessing and spiritual enrichment unseen and unthought of by you.

Remember the Fatherhood of God.

A visitor at a school for the deaf and dumb was writing questions on the blackboard for the children. By and by he wrote this sentence: "Why has God made me to hear and speak, and made you deaf and dumb?" The awful sentence fell upon the little ones like a fierce blow in the face. They sat palsied before that dreadful *why*. And then a little girl arose. Her lip was trembling. Her eyes were swimming with tears. Straight to the board she walked, and, picking up the crayon wrote with firm hand these precious words: *"Even so, Father, for so it seemed*

good in Thy sight." What a reply! It reaches up and lays
hold of an eternal truth upon which the maturest believer
as well as the youngest child of God may alike unshakably
rest—the truth that *God is your Father.* Do you mean
that? Do you really and fully believe that? When you do,
then your dove of faith will no longer wander in weary
unrest, but will settle down forever in its eternal resting
place of peace. *"Your Father!"* Why, that takes in everything! Because He is your Father, how *could* He fail or
forget you? Look into your own father heart and mark
the strength, the tenderness, the unspeakableness of your
love for that winsome little one enshrined in your heart
of hearts. Then say to yourself, "God's Father love for
me infinitely surpasses all this." Your Father! Against
that all doubts must at last dash themselves to pieces as
the sea spray beats itself to nothingness upon a rock-
bound coast. Down upon that your child-trained soul
will find a final resting place in untrembling trustfulness.
Rear that up before the devil's subtle, hideous, hissing
why; and he will stagger back, the unmasked, baffled,
beaten traitor that in truth he is.

THE NUTSHELL OF PROPHECY

Then was the secret revealed unto Daniel in a night vision.
DANIEL 2:19

Nebuchadnezzar the king of Babylon had dreamed a strange dream. In it he had seen a great image with its motley fashioning of gold, silver, brass, iron, and clay. Then the dream had slipped from his treacherous memory. Straightway he called his magicians and threatened them with death unless they both recalled the dream and gave its interpretation. The Chaldeans were thrown into a panic. In the midst of it all God revealed the vision and its meaning to His beloved servant Daniel. At once Daniel is brought into the presence of the king and calls back to him the forgotten dream. Here are his inspired words to the king (chap. 2):

31 Thou, O king, sawest, and behold a great image. This great image, whose brightness was excellent, stood before thee; and the form thereof was terrible.
32 This image's head was of fine gold, his breast and his arms of silver, his belly and his thighs of brass,
33 His legs of iron, his feet part of iron and part of clay.
34 Thou sawest till that a stone was cut out without hands, which smote the image upon his feet that were of iron and clay, and brake them to pieces.
35 Then was the iron, the clay, the brass, the silver, and the gold, broken to pieces together, and became like the chaff of the summer threshing floors; and the wind carried them away, that no place was found for them: and the stone that smote the image became a great mountain, and filled the whole earth.

It is a wondrously simple picture.

Many think the image is strange, grotesque, and difficult of understanding. Its make-up of gold, silver, brass, iron, and clay seems to them mysterious and complicated. On the contrary it is luminously simple. It was given by God to a Babylonian king. Its imagery was just the kind the Babylonians were familiar with in the images and symbols of their tablets, walls, and monuments. It is a real kindergarten picture. Its thought-grooves are so easy to follow that any intelligent child can understand it. Indeed, it is just the kind of a story you would like to tell to a child in the glow and shadow-play of an open fire. And the child would grasp it too. The only reason we ourselves do not is that we approach it with a mind like cement so hardened and set in the matrix of a traditional interpretation that we actually cannot receive the impression which the story, just as God has told it, would make upon a plastic child-mind.

This image is a history of Gentile kingdoms from their beginning to their end.

Israel had disobeyed God to the final limit. She had proved utterly faithless and willful in her rejection of His law and His tender love. So God carries out His oft-repeated pledge that He would cast her off and scatter her among the nations. He takes the kingdom from her and sets up the Gentile kingdoms to rule the world during the time of her rejection. Of these world-kingdoms Nebuchadnezzar, king of Babylon, was the first head, and Babylon the first kingdom (2:37-38):

> 37 Thou, O king, art a king of kings: for the God of heaven hath given thee a kingdom.
> 38 Thou art this head of gold.

Nothing could be clearer than this. The Babylonian is the first of these Gentile world-kingdoms. Then follow the other kingdoms in succession (2:39-40):

39 And after thee shall arise another kingdom inferior to thee, and another third kingdom of brass, which shall bear rule over all the earth.

40 And the fourth kingdom shall be strong as iron: forasmuch as iron breaketh in pieces and subdueth all things.

Secular history gives us the narrative of these other kingdoms precisely as divine prophecy has here depicted it. For after Babylon came the second world-kingdom, the Medo-Persian. Then came the third, the Grecian kingdom under Alexander the Great. Lastly arose the fourth, the Roman kingdom with its iron strength and endurance. In simple diagram the image's picture-story of these kingdoms is as follows:

Head of Gold	The Babylonian Kingdom
Breast of Silver	The Medo-Persian Kingdom
Thighs of Brass	The Grecian Kingdom
Legs and Feet of Iron	The Roman Kingdom

The symbolism of the two legs, which indicate the division of the image, was exactly fulfilled in the division of the Roman empire into the Eastern and Western empires. And these empires finally dwindled into the smaller kingdoms pictured in the toes of the image which represent in kind, though not yet in number, the remnants of the original Roman empire as they exist today in the regions originally occupied by that great kingdom. What a marvelous proof that "holy men of old spake as they were moved by the Holy Ghost" to see here one of God's prophets narrating twenty-five centuries ago the rise and course of Gentile governments with an orderly succession and fulness of detail which the historian looking back over those twenty-five centuries pronounces to be unerringly accurate.

This image-vision is also the nutshell of New Testament prophecy.

We have seen what a wondrous history it is of the Gentile world kingdoms up to this present hour. But it is more than that. For it is also the nutshell of New Testament prophecy. It is like Rome's golden milestone. From it the great highways of unfulfilled prophecy take their start. How true this is we shall see as we proceed to consider further the language of the vision (2:34-35), as also that of chapter 7.

> 34 Thou sawest till that a stone was cut out without hands, which smote the image upon his feet that were of iron and clay, and brake them to pieces.
> 35 Then was the iron, the clay, the brass, the silver, and the gold, broken to pieces together, and became like the chaff of the summer threshing floors; and the wind carried them away, that no place was found for them: and the stone that smote the image became a great mountain, and filled the whole earth.

7:7-8

> 7 After this I saw in the night visions, and behold a fourth beast, dreadful and terrible, and strong exceedingly; and it had great iron teeth: it devoured and brake in pieces, and stamped the residue with the feet of it: and it was diverse from all the beasts that were before it; and it had ten horns.
> 8 I considered the horns, and, behold, there came up among them another little horn, before whom there were three of the first horns plucked up by the roots; and, behold, in this horn were eyes like the eyes of man, and a mouth speaking great things.

Now, concerning the image and its parallel vision of chapter 7, note this fact: there are four simple, striking object pictures—all of which are concrete symbols having a clear prophetic teaching—which make up the nutshell of unfulfilled prophecy of the New Testament. These objects are (1) the feet and toes, (2) the horn, (3) the stone, and (4) the mountain.

The parts of the great image, namely, head, breast, thighs, and legs, all, as we have seen, represent successive world kingdoms. So also the feet and toes, which are the last division of the image, plainly indicate the final division which the Gentile world kingdoms shall reach. It is upon the feet and the toes that the stone cut out of the mountain strikes and destroys the image, proving that the toes are the last divisions of world empire just as the undivided head of gold was the first. All doubt as to this truth is removed by the evidence in the seventh chapter. There Daniel had another vision. In it he sees four great beasts come up from the sea (v. 3). These four beasts stand for the four kingdoms which were seen before in the picture of the great image. The fourth beast is distinctly stated to be "the fourth kingdom upon earth" (v. 23), which we have just seen to be Rome.

> 23 Thus he said, The fourth beast shall be the fourth kingdom upon earth, which shall be diverse from all kingdoms, and shall devour the whole earth, and shall tread it down, and break it in pieces.
> 24 And the ten horns out of this kingdom are ten kings that shall arise.

This fourth beast has ten horns (v. 7). And these ten horns are declared (v. 24) to be "ten kings that shall arise" out of this kingdom. Thus the last division of Rome into the ten toes is paralleled by its division into ten horns, and these are clearly declared to be ten kings, with their kingdoms. Hence the scriptural proof is clear that the last stage of Gentile world kingdoms will be reached when the territory covered by ancient Rome becomes a confederation of ten kings and kingdoms. It is "in the days of these kings" that the stone smites and "the God of heaven sets up a kingdom which shall never be destroyed" (2:44). From this concrete symbol of the toes of the image therefore emerges this first great prophetic teaching of the image, namely that the last stage of human world kingdoms will be a group of ten kings with their kingdoms, which grouping of the nations will foretoken the end.

The horn has eyes like a man's.

This grouping, into the significant number of ten, of the kingdoms which cover the territory once occupied by ancient Rome, will be the great political sign which foreruns the end of the age. When "they that are wise" see it they will understand that it means the end of Gentile world government is near at hand. But before the end comes to these kingdoms something significant takes place among them. The Word of God now gives us the picture of a striking internal development in the story of these ten kingdoms. It is found in 7:7-8, 24:

> After this I saw a fourth beast. And it had ten horns.
> 8 I considered the horns, and, behold, there came up among them another little horn, before whom there were three of the first horns plucked up by the roots: and, behold, in this horn were eyes like the eyes of man, and a mouth speaking great things.
> 24 And the ten horns out of this kingdom are ten kings that shall arise: and another shall rise after them; and he shall be diverse from the first, and he shall subdue three kings.

The fourth beast, we note again, has ten horns. There comes up among them another "little horn." Before him three of the first horns are "plucked up by the roots." Verse 24 tells us exactly what all this means. The ten horns are ten kings. The other horn which rises among them is another king. He overcomes three of the first kings. In this little horn are "eyes like the eyes of man." He is a great, outstanding man among these other ten kingdom heads. All this is here clearly interpreted. In a sentence it is this: Before the end of these last ten kingdoms a superman shall arise who will conquer three of them and occupy a place of dominating control and power over the group. Is there any mention elsewhere in the Scriptures of a phenomenal man arising who shall be a towering figure in world history and world-government and be another great sign which betokens the nearing end? The Holy Spirit's answer to this, through the apostle Paul, is startling.

Speaking of this very end Paul (2 Th 2:3) says, "That day shall not come, except that man of sin be revealed."

Revelation 13 gives a full-length portrait of this "little horn," or "man of sin," which nearly all prophetical scholars take to be the portrait of the Antichrist. Verse 18 says, "Let him that hath understanding count the number of the beast: for it is the number of a man."

Thus Daniel, Paul, and John picture the coming of this sinister man of wickedness and power as one of the great prophetic figures marking the end of the age. The next great truth which finds its birthplace in this Daniel nutshell of prophecy is that in the last group of these Gentile kingdoms there shall arise as overlord a king of such unprecedented wickedness that the Word of God calls him "the man of sin," otherwise known as the Antichrist or "the lawless one."

The stone strikes the swift blow.

The world kingdoms reach this significant number of ten. The internal political changes put the man of sin in the dominating place of kingship. Then comes a picture of the third great prophetic truth. A swift, sudden, supernatural ("without hands") blow falls upon the man of sin and his world kingdoms and they are annihilated. So complete is the destruction that the Word of God compares them to the "chaff of the summer threshing floor" which is tossed into the air to be carried away by the summer winds. There is only one great coming event which in its suddenness, power, and overwhelming results can possibly fulfill this picture. It is the second coming in glory of our Lord Jesus Christ. We have just seen clearly that the Man of Sin and his kingdom are destroyed at

114

the age-end. But we also read (2 Th 2:8) that at Christ's coming the Man of Sin is "destroyed by the brightness of His coming." This is clear, logical, and Scriptural proof that the great coming event which ends these world kingdoms and their overlord is the Second Advent of our Lord Jesus Christ. Moreover, in the picture in Revelation 19 of Jesus Christ's coming again we see this Man of Sin there entitled "the beast" and "the kings of the earth and their armies gathered together to make war against him that sat upon the horse." And it is then and there at the age-end, that they are overthrown by the Lord coming in His glory. Thus the glorious coming again of our Lord Jesus Christ is the focal center to which all New Testament prophecies converge and this is the swift, sudden blow which at the end shatters the Gentile world kingdoms.

The mountain fills the earth.

The image stands for human kingdoms.
The image is succeeded by the kingdom of heaven.
The image is crushed by the coming of Christ.
Thus we have the whole story. This kingdom of heaven is not an improvement of earthly kingdoms. It is a replacement of them. There is no "christianizing" of these last kingdoms of the earth, no betterment of their quality and character which will permit the God of heaven to use them under His Son in the ruling of the world. They are simply annihilated. They vanish away as utterly as "the chaff of the summer threshing floor" which is tossed into the wind and disappears so completely that no place is found for it (Dan 2:35). That the kingdom which is then set up is God's kingdom; that it destroys all the other kingdoms; that it shall never be destroyed, but shall last forever is clearly and explicitly stated in verse 44: "And in the days of these kings shall the God of heaven set up a kingdom which shall never be destroyed: and the kingdom shall not be left to other people, but it shall break in pieces and consume all these kingdoms, and it

shall stand for ever." Moreover that this kingdom is the kingdom of the coming Christ is just as clearly stated in Daniel 7:13-14:

> 13 I saw in the night visions, and, behold, one like the Son of man came with the clouds of heaven, and came to the Ancient of days, and they brought him near before him.
> 14 And there was given him dominion, and glory, and a kingdom, that all people, nations, and languages, should serve him: his dominion is an everlasting dominion, which shall not pass away, and his kingdom that which shall not be destroyed.

The last great prophetic truth therefore which we discover in this Daniel nutshell of prophecy is that there can be no kingdom without a king, and only when the King of Glory comes and ends the world kingdoms will the God of Heaven set up a kingdom which shall fill the whole earth and shall last forever.

Thus four great highways of prophecy concerning the things yet to come lead out from this second chapter of Daniel into and through the pages of the New Testament culminating in the wondrous book of Revelation. These things yet to come are the end of Gentile kingdoms, the man of sin, the King of Glory, and the Kingdom of Heaven.

The man who studies this scripture and sees two thousand five hundred years of prophecy unroll into certified history, unerring in its most minute detail, will, if he is wise, come to the conclusion that God is the only one who "knows the end from the beginning"; that this Word of His is the one infallible witness to the coming end; and that in it as the children of God, "We have also a more sure word of prophecy; whereunto ye do well that ye take heed, as unto a light that shineth in a dark place, until the day dawn, and the day star arise in your hearts." (2 Pe 1:19).

THE BLESSED HOPE

Looking for that blessed hope, and the glorious appearing of the great God and our Saviour Jesus Christ.

TITUS 2:13

One summer morning we were awakened at a very early hour. The first faint flush of dawn was painting the horizon. Back of the mountain summit a strange light was shining. As seen through the patches of foliage in the treetops it seemed like a brilliant electric arc light. The swaying leaves caused it to shimmer and gleam, appear and disappear with puzzling regularity. By and by it reached the sky line. As it tipped the treetops a stray telephone wire moved across its face, bisecting it like the cross hair of a telescope. In a moment it had shaken itself free, even from this partner, and stood out sharp and clear in all its beauty above the scarp of the mountain. And then as it flooded the scene with light like molten silver we recognized the daystar. Never had it seemed so large, so radiant, so flooded with glory as when it broke forth from the forest that summer morning in a new and strange place to us, and with unfamiliar and unaccustomed surroundings.

So, emerging from the pages of this Book of God, is the splendid truth of the return of our Lord and Saviour, Jesus Christ, to this earth. It shines with the coming glory of Him who says of Himself, "I am the bright and morning star." Prejudice and dullness of spiritual vision have hidden it from the eyes of multitudes. But the cross hairs of God's telescope of prophecy are centered upon it as the supreme and absorbing event of the end of this age. It has grown in beauty and radiance to God's own children until now it fills the horizon of their thought and expectation as never before, and God calls upon us to be "looking for that blessed hope, and the glorious appearing of the great God and our Saviour, Jesus Christ" (Titus 2:13).

It is the hope of the Word.

Throughout the entire New Testament the one supreme hope to which the heart and mind of the believer is constantly turned is the return of his Lord and his own glorification with Him. We cite but a few of the many passages pointing to it:

> Looking for that blessed hope, and the glorious appearing of the great God and our Saviour Jesus Christ (Titus 2:13).
> Your life is hid with Christ in God. When Christ, who is our life, shall appear, then shall ye also appear with him in glory (Col 3:3-4).
> Beloved, now are we the sons of God, and it doth not yet appear what we shall be: but we know that, when he shall appear, we shall be like him; for we shall see him as he is. And every man that hath this hope in him purifieth himself (1 Jn 3:2-3).
> Unto them that look for him shall he appear the second time without sin unto salvation (Heb 9:28).
> This same Jesus, which is taken up from you into heaven, shall so come in like manner as ye have seen him go into heaven (Ac 1:11).
> And, behold, I come quickly; and my reward is with me, to give every man according as his work shall be (Rev 22:12).
> Behold, he cometh with clouds; and every eye shall see him (Rev 1:7).

It is the hope of the heart.

Many years have passed since the slaves of the British West Indian colonies were emancipated. Historians tell a beautiful story of this momentous event. The day set for the emancipation was the first day of August. The night before, many of the slaves, it is said, never slept at all. Their hearts were so eager with expectation that they could not close their eyes. Thousands of them gathered in their places of worship for prayer and praise to God for bringing to them their freedom. Some of their brethren were sent to the nearby hilltops to view the first gleams of the coming dawn. These reported by signal to the waiting ones below when the dawn of the fateful and jubilant day was breaking. Day of all days was it to them, when they should pass from the thralldom of human ownership to the liberty and independence of the new life. Who can picture the hope that thrilled their innermost hearts as they watched for the dawn of that day.

Likewise a great emancipation day is coming for the children of God. The enthrallment of sin is to be broken forever; infirmities are to give place to infinities; corruption is to be changed to incorruption; mortality is to clothe itself with immortality; feeble and changeable fellowship is to be transmuted into endless and unbroken communion with our Lord; limitation and imperfection of service is to give way to boundlessness and perfectness of ministry throughout all eternity. And all this is to come with the coming of the Lord Jesus Christ.

Now the supreme and unerring witness of the coming of our Lord is the Word of God. The Spirit tells us (2 Pe 1:19) that "we have also a more sure word of prophecy; whereunto ye do well that ye take heed."

To this word of prophecy we are to take earnest heed. As we brood, meditate, and pray over it, the blessed hope will become increasingly real and precious to our souls. And the witness of the Word of God is, as we have seen, most clear and emphatic as to this great truth. But by and by is to come another witness. For we are admonished in the same verse above that we are to take heed to this word of prophecy until a certain time. Until when? "Until the day dawn, and the day star arise in your hearts." Jesus Christ is the Daystar. "I am the bright and morning star," He says of Himself.

These West Indian slaves, when they saw the first streaks of dawn of their day of freedom, sent back witnesses to their fellows that the long looked for moment was at hand. So, just before Jesus appears, the witness in the Word to the blessed hope will culminate in a special witness in the heart. Just before He comes, God will give to us an overwhelmingly jubilant, intense consciousness that Jesus is about to break forth from the heavens which have so long contained Him. The Spirit of Christ within will witness to our spirit that the moment has arrived. The daystar will arise in our hearts as the forerunning witness of His rising in the heavens. God will give to us a fore-thrill, as it were, of the power of the Spirit of glory which in a moment more shall transform the bodies of our humiliation into the likeness of the body of His glory.

It is the hope of heaven.

"Being the children of the resurrection" (Lk 20:36).

Do you remember our Lord's wondrous statement about these resurrection bodies when the Sadducees tried to entrap Him by one of their foolish questions? They had supposed the case of a woman having seven husbands in succession, and then sought to bring Him to confusion before the multitude by asking Him whose wife she would be in the resurrection. Back came His marvelous teaching that in heaven there would be neither marrying nor giving in marriage, but that all of God's children would be "children of the resurrection." Do you note that striking phrase and its significance? Plainly it is this: Marriage was given by God for the perpetuation of the race. Through its holy relationship children are born into the world with their natural bodies. The pangs of birth and the long, slow years of growth fashion these natural bodies of ours. But neither marriage, nor natural birth, nor the long progress of years will be needed to fashion the new, glorified bodies of His redeemed children.

That body is fashioned in an instant, the glory-instant of the resurrection. It needs no human union for its creation. It leaps into being at the supernatural touch of God's resurrection power. Heaven shall be filled with a race of beings, who, as to the body, will flash into it in a second of time, "in a moment, in the twinkling of an eye." It shall be peopled with millions of glorious bodies of God's children. Thus they are "children of the resurrection." And heaven itself is waiting for the blessed hope of the Lord's coming which shall bring to it myriads of its children whose new bodies are swift-born by the Spirit of God from the womb of the resurrection of glory.

It is the hope of creation.

"For the earnest expectation of the creature waiteth" (Ro 8:19).

"The creature itself also shall be delivered from the bondage of corruption" (Ro 8:21).

God rears the mighty oak through years of patient growth, yet though it stands for centuries it crumbles at the last under the touch of time and decay. God fashions the lilies in all their grace of contour and stainlessness of white; yet they nod and sway for but a few passing days until corruption withers and lays them low. God carpets the midsummer field with miles of pink and fragrant cloverbloom, but decay prostrates it in sere and blackened death upon its mother earth. All of nature's beauty and grace which the spring breeze breathes upon in its unspeakable loveliness, the winter winds find lying in death and hopeless decay. But the creation is to be delivered from this bondage of corruption into the "glorious liberty of the sons of God." As the sons of God shall be set free from death and corruption, so also shall nature. She shall blossom and bloom in perennial beauty and undecaying glory. The earth itself is to share the deathlessness of God's own children.

Hence the beautiful personification of the physical creation itself "waiting for the revelation of the sons of God" because that creation itself is to be delivered from the same

121

limitation of death and corruption that now fetters and hampers the physical being of the sons of God themselves. The flower shall no longer fade; the grass shall no longer wither and be cast into the oven; the giant oak shall not then crumble into the dust of decay. No wonder then that "the earnest expectation of the creature waiteth for the manifestation of the sons of God" (Ro 8:19). For when Jesus shall come again physical creation shall share the same glorious deliverance from death and corruption which come to God's own.

The exact thought of John 1:11 is: "He came unto His own (things), and His own (people) received him not." The sea yielded to Him and bore His sacred feet in triumphant disregard of all its laws. The fish crowded into the nets of His disciples at His word of command. The loaves changed, and multiplied, and fed the perishing thousands as He broke them. The winds ceased from their wild and boisterous sway as He spoke to them. The sea ceased to rage and threaten His fearful followers and sank into peace and quiet when He spake. All His creation received their Lord and confessed His power. But His own people received Him not. So here. There is a touch of pathos in this word that the whole creation of God is waiting for the coming of His Son while that hope has slipped from the hearts of so many of His people.

It is a blessed hope.

The man who cherishes this hope at once throws himself open in the popular mind to the charge of pessimism. Men say he looks upon all things with sober, sombre view. There are no sun-tipped mountain peaks of promise for him; all is shrouded in darkness and gloom. But there could be no greater mistake. For the Word of God calls the hope of the Lord's return a "blessed hope." That is a "happy" hope, as the word literally means. It brings joy to the heart of the believer. It gladdens the soul of him who cherishes it. For there is no truer optimist than the man who is looking for his Lord to come.

True, he, as none else, realizes that dark and perilous times are coming. His Guidebook warns him there are breakers ahead for this old world of ours. He knows that Jesus Christ's statement about it is not that it is growing better, but that "the whole world lieth in the evil one" and is rapidly nearing the fiercest crisis of all its history. But none of these things move him. Being forewarned he is forearmed. And being forearmed he knows no discouragement because of conditions or circumstances.

For back of all the sombre shadows of coming days looms up the glorious figure of his coming Lord and King, whose victory is as certain as the eternal Word of God can declare, and the love of God can bring to pass. His hope is therefore indeed a blessed hope. It is sure and steadfast. It steadies his heart amid the most trying, desperate circumstances. And it inspires him to service, too, with new zeal and fidelity. For that this blessed hope of the Lord's return "cuts the nerve of service" is but another of the manifest fallacies which find birth in the theories of its critics instead of the lives of its lovers. Nothing could be farther from the truth. It stimulates to fervent zeal and earnestness for lost souls as they who cherish it do well know.

Almost to a man the great evangelist and soul-winners of the age are lovers and preachers of the blessed hope. Spurgeon, Moody, Chapman, Torrey, Sunday, Whittle, all have cherished with warm and earnest hearts the hope of their Lord's return. The greatest coterie of Bible teachers this continent has ever seen, the men of the famous Niagara Bible Conference, were given up wholly and fervently to this truth. Brookes, Scofield, Erdman, Moorehead, and Parsons—every man of this quintet of princely teachers found joy in believing and in propagating this blessed truth. And not only these, but thousands of God's messengers on the mission field testify to it as one of the mighty inspirations of their lives to eager, incessant service. If that great truth makes daydreamers and stargazers of men, then it is strange indeed to find Jesus Christ Himself exhorting His own, as they serve, to be "like unto men that wait for their lord" (Lk 12:36).

It is a purifying hope.

"He that hath this hope in him purifieth himself" (1 Jn 3:3).

Years ago we were standing with a friend on the deck of a great ship. We had both been abroad for a year. And now our ship's prow was pointed toward the homeland. As we stood we talked of the wondrous sights of that memorable year. We saw again the glory of Switzerland's sun-tipped peaks; we heard the murmurous surf of the Mediterranean; we walked through famous galleries and feasted our eyes upon paintings and statues of worldwide fame and matchless beauty; we stood upon lofty mountain summits where the whole world seemed to lie at our feet; we wandered by the banks of lakes and inland seas which would be a neverending dream of loveliness in all the years to come. As the moments went by, the more we talked, the more enthusiastic we grew. But we were forgetting something. It was the homeland. We needed something to turn our hearts thitherward. And presently it came.

God laid His hand upon sea and sky in one of the most gorgeous sunsets our mortal eyes had ever beheld. A lake of gold, fringed with meadows of blue, lay embosomed on the evening sky. Above it overarching clouds flooded with silver radiance formed a gateway through which the setting sun poured the splendid light of parting day. Through this gateway in the golden west our good ship seemed to be sailing onward. And then came a rush of joy unspeakable. Back of the golden gateway of glory through which we were sailing was home! Then a great hope swept into our hearts. It was a hope that went out to the homeland, and the dear ones there. And as it laid hold upon us with imperious sway everything else was swept out. The beauties of Italy and Switzerland were forgotten in the unspeakable joy of hope. And we learned that day as never before the searching, separating, expulsive power of a blessed hope.

So it is with us who are God's children. We are drawn unconsciously into the swift stream of the world's thought, activity, and power. We live, move, and toil amid intensely worldly surroundings. Engrossed in these we forget something. We forget that it is the things which are unseen that are eternal. So God thrusts into the horizon of our daily thought and meditation this blessed hope of our Lord's return. And amazing indeed is its separating power in the life. It is an otherworldly truth. With a tremendous tug upward, it lays hold upon our thought and spirit. It has a special blessing pronounced upon its study (Rev 1:3). And any child of God who comes to know and love it is at once conscious of the nature of that blessing. Its searchingness and effectiveness in separating us from the power of worldliness in our lives is astonishing to us as we realize how vain our own self-efforts have been to accomplish this longed-for result. This wondrous power to purify and detach the heart from worldly engrossment is convincing proof that it is God's divinely appointed truth for effecting that purpose in the hearts and lives of His children. In very truth is it that "he hath this hope in him purifieth himself, even as he is pure."

It is the only hope of victory.

Picture to yourself a great kingdom belonging to a wise and loving king. That king goes away for a long absence bidding his people to occupy until he comes again. While he is absent a strong, hostile king is in possession of the land. That false king is Satan. He holds most cruel and tyrannical sway over the people of the land. Hating with relentless hatred the true king, he ravages the country with all the malignant power he can command. With

125

fiendish hatred he injects into the blood of the people a deadly poison. That poison is sin. Think of the awful havoc of sin in this world of ours. "By one man sin entered" (Ro 5:12). That was an awful entrance! Heaven must have wept tears of agony, and perdition held fiendish jubilee on that black day when "by one man sin entered."

And what a record it has made! It has swept like a mighty tidal wave for centuries over a world engulfed in its black depths; who shall stay its flood? It has scorched and consumed like a volcano of flame all that have felt its fiery touch; who shall extinguish its fires? It has eaten like a great canker into the very vitals of all human life; who shall find a healing ointment for its leprous touch? It has stabbed to the innermost heart the innocent and the guilty alike; who shall quench the crimson streams which gush from its murderous wound? And this deadly virus in the soul ceases not from its ruinous work until it has destroyed the body also.

For as by one man sin entered, so also came "death through sin." Sin follows in the wake of Satan; death follows in the trail of sin. And what a monster foe he is. He baffles our plans; he blasts our hopes; he withers our strength; he fills our cup of sorrow to the full, and, until Jesus comes, he brings down into the dust of decay and corruption the mortal body of every being that walks God's beautiful earth. Thrice in every century does he sweep a thousand millions of human beings from life to death, from mortality to corruption.

What think you? Can final victory ever come to this earth until this false, usurping king is cast out; this deadly malady of sin healed; and this ruin of body and souls of myriads ended? Surely not. And the final victory over this deadly trio of foes, Satan, sin, and death, is to be won by the coming and personal presence of our Lord Jesus Christ. Nor does this imply any failure of the work of the Holy Spirit in this Gospel age. God never designed that He should finish the work which Jesus alone can complete. The Spirit may deliver us from the power of Satan, but only Christ can banish Satan from this earth. The Spirit may break the mastership of sin in our lives, but only Christ can drive sin from the earth. The Spirit may give us solace and comfort under the stroke of death, but He will never exile that dread foe from this world. All this is the triumphant work of our Lord Jesus Christ, who will conquer Satan, banish sin, and tread death under foot only after He Himself shall come again to reign in righteousness and universal peace.